THE ENTREPRENEUR

WHITE BALL THINKING

PART ONE

DESIGNOVATION: THE PROCESS FOR BRINGING PLANS INTO REALITY.

BY D.F.MCKEEVER

AMAZON EDITION

ISBN:9781791697778

COPYRIGHT 2011 D.F.MCKEEVER

DISCLAIMER & PRIVACY POLICY THIS BOOK IS LICENSED FOR YOUR PERSONAL ENJOYMENT ONLY. THIS IS THE SOLE PROPERTY OF DESIGNOVATION. ALL RIGHTS ARE RESERVED. NO PART OF THIS WORK MAY BE REPRODUCED OR TRANSMITTED IN ANY FORM OR BY ANY MEANS; ELECTRONIC OR MECHANICAL, INCLUDING, PHOTOCOPYING, RECORDING OR BY ANY INFORMATION STORAGE OR RETRIEVAL SYSTEM, WITHOUT THE WRITTEN PERMISSION OF THE COPYRIGHT OWNER. DESIGNOVATION SHALL NOT BE HELD LIABLE TO ANY PERSON OR ENTITY WITH RESPECT TO ANY LOSS OR DAMAGE CAUSED OR ALLEGED TO BE CAUSED DIRECTLY OR INDIRECTLY BY THE INFORMATION CONTAINED WITHIN THIS WORK. FURTHERMORE, NO PART OF THIS MAY BE REPRINTED OR RESOLD. THIS EBOOK MAY NOT BE RE-SOLD OR GIVEN AWAY TO OTHER PEOPLE. IF YOU WOULD LIKE TO SHARE THIS BOOK WITH ANOTHER PERSON, PLEASE PURCHASE AN ADDITIONAL COPY FOR EACH RECIPIENT. IF YOU'RE READING THIS BOOK AND DID NOT PURCHASE IT, OR IT WAS NOT PURCHASED FOR YOUR USE ONLY, THEN PLEASE RETURN TO KINDLEBOOKS.COM THANK YOU FOR RESPECTING THE WORK OF THIS AUTHOR.

LEARN MORE:

HTTP://WWW.DESIGNOVATION.CO.UK

https://youtu.be/uwp7A3U_5hs

*"This is for all the dreamers out there
who through adversity and faith
still hope for a greater future!"*

This book is dedicated to my Grandmother
Mary Burns 23rd Sept 1920- 2014
(Parts of this book are factual relating to my grandmothers early childhood & married life in both Ireland and Scotland. My Grand mother & Grand father met working as a kitchen hand and footman for Lord David Sterling the founder of SAS at Keir House before the outbreak of the Second World War.)

Contents

	Page
Introduction	6
Chapter 1 Keir House 1941, Scotland	9
Chapter 2 The World's Creativity Park 2061, Glasgow	17
Chapter 3 Home	29
Chapter 4 The Inverted Atrium	39
Chapter 5 The White Ball introduction	43
Chapter 6 *I The Spirit*	46
Chapter 7 The Inspirational Garden	55
Chapter 8 *II The Believer*	62
Chapter 9 The Library	68
Chapter 10 *III The Designer*	76
Chapter 11 The Dream Room	85
Chapter 12 *IV The Inventor*	91
Chapter 13 The Designovation ® Studio	100
Chapter 14 *V The Gambler*	113
Chapter 15 The Great Pioneers	119

	Page
Chapter 16 *VI The Rebel*	126
Chapter 17 The Time Machine	133
Chapter 18 The Future	140
The Summary	143
Notes	146
Bibliography	154

Introduction

I am 40 years of age and live happily in my home town in Scotland. My family and friends would best describe me as a creative introvert and passionate optimist with an unconventional career in the creative fields and business. My passions in life are studying business, personal development & creative entrepreneurs. My life long fascination of business and creative individuals began on my first vacation to Florida aged 15, when my father gave me my first personal development book 'Think and grow Rich' by Napoleon Hill when visiting the home of one of the worlds most creative Entrepreneurs Walt Disney.

Life has come full circle and 25 years on and returning from a vacation with my young family in Disney World Florida I find myself compelled to write this, my first book. Even though I consider myself a poor communicator and English student I find it necessary to try this medium to share my ideas and thoughts with others. This book is my 'paying it forward' to my children and a new generation of dreamers and entrepreneurs. Like Napoleon Hill

25 years ago, I hope my thoughts and stories offer others the inspiration to believe in their dreams.

This is Part One of two unique and innovative books of both non-fiction and fiction designed to fully engage the reader during two different periods in history with two separate but interlinked philosophies 'Black Box' and 'White Ball' thinking known as the 'Designovation ®' philosophy. Over the years I have realised that in both conventional business books and personal development books one of the most essential ingredients of any great individual, entrepreneur or enterprise is either neglected or rarely discussed. The same essential ingredient is responsible for creating solutions, progress, innovation & economic growth.

This ingredient is present at the inception of any career or business but eventually vanishes as the person or business matures resulting often in stagnation. Occasionally it survives beyond inception to become an integral ingredient to the life of an individual, entrepreneur or enterprise namely 'Creativity'. Through my contradicting life experiences in both the creative and business worlds I believe you can harness and teach the skill of creativity through the Designovation ® principles. Creativity has 6 key characteristics which I define as White ball thinking. I believe these same 6 shared characteristics are reflective in the lives or enterprises of some of the world's greats i.e. Walt Disney, James Dyson, Andrew Carnegie, Dame Anita Roddick, and Sir Richard Branson.

This book is the first in a series of books introducing the various elements of the Designovation ® principles and demonstrates how with creativity everyone has the potential to achieve sustained growth, innovation and a new ethical approach to business.

"The passionate are the only advocates who always persuade. The simplest man (or woman) with passion will be more persuasive than the most eloquent without." Rene Descartes

Chapter 1

Keir House 1941, Scotland

It was a bitter cold evening, Mary & Duncan huddled together as they sat in the kitchen, in front of the warm roaring fire with the room filled with the scent of smoky charred wood. They sat talking with excitement about their wedding plans and future life together. The recent announcement of their engagement came as no surprise to the owners and staff at Keir House. Unfortunately it was only a few days until Duncan would be leaving Scotland for his RAF post in England and like many young couples their wedding plans would have to be postponed and planned around the constraints and demands of the War. As they spoke they could hear in the background the faint brisk sound of foot steps approaching. This soon followed by the sound of the large kitchen door and its rusty hinges squeaking open.

"Oh there you are Duncan, I've been looking for you both everywhere, both of you stay there" said the Butler anxiously, as he about turned and made his way back down the hallway.

Mary & Duncan looked at each other hesitantly. Momentarily the Butler returned, shortly followed by the sound of women's footsteps. Mary & Duncan quickly and instinctively stood up as the Lady of the House appeared at the doorway with a brown leather bound book held tightly to her chest while clutching a small brown leather pouch. Before entering the room the Lady scanned the hallway behind her, to ensure no one had followed her and then closed the door firmly behind her.

"We have just received news of a potential air attack and possible land attack via the North Sea, the country is on high alert. I need the both of you to follow my instructions and collect all the family silverware from the banquet room and set off and bury it on the Estate, you both must go now" she said firmly to Duncan & the Butler.

"Yes Mam! " Duncan nodded respectfully, glancing at the Butler, Duncan exited the kitchen as the Butler followed closely behind, closing the kitchen door quietly ensuring not to disturb anyone else in the house.

The Lady looked at Mary and taking her hand guided her to the fireplace where she sat down in Cook's cracked and worn leather chair, nodding to

Mary to sit down on the wooden bench next to her. Mary sat nervously and attentively.

At only 21 years of age Mary stood out from the other employees at Keir House. As an Irish immigrant who had come to Scotland aged 19 years old, her passionate spirit and work ethic instantly struck a chord with the Lady. She was different in so many ways from all the other staff at Keir House. Mary had a creative resourcefulness, common sense and a tireless work ethic, but most of all her confidence and assertiveness to challenge and question authority made it impossible for her to go unnoticed. The Lady of the house admired Mary's passionate drive, youth and optimism but slightly envied her freedom to challenge conformity as a working class girl.

"Mary I have thought long and hard about this I have no grand daughters and do not know what will be the outcome of this War. Therefore I would like you to have a gift that has been with my family through the decades. Times are changing and I know intuitively that it is only right that this gift is shared with those of another class and generation, in the hope it may achieve its intended purpose, I want you to have this." said the Lady, gently placing the brown leather bound book and pouch into Mary's hands.

Mary looked at the book and pouch with surprise and hesitance due to the unusual circumstance of the unfolding events.

"Inside this pouch is only one of two original paper weights, a white glass ball." The Lady bent over and opened the small leather pouch to reveal a white glass ball paper weight. "This book which accompanies the paper weight is a book of two valuable teachings, made up of two halves part one is about *creative power* and the *'white ball principles'*, part two is about *material power* and something known as the *'black box principles'*. The original wooden black box paper weight along with a summary of the black box principles (thought to be the original book) was kept by the male elders in our family. Unfortunately it was taken from the estate many years ago and was said to have been given to a young man who left to seek his fortunes in America. No one is aware of the existence of the white ball paper weight or the original book in its entirety with its 'white ball' principles as it has never been revealed to anyone. It has been kept a secret through the centuries between the women in our family with each grandmother passing it down to the eldest granddaughter of each generation. My mother always maintained that the most valuable of the teachings and paper weights lay in the secrets of the white ball and its principles which are about the human spirit and creative power which has unlimited timeless power when combined with the black box principles. "

Mary listened attentively as the Lady of the House continued.

"I am entrusting this gift with you because I do not know how this War is going to unfold. I am going to break with tradition because we need change I believe in my heart I can entrust this gift with you and in your lifetime you can decide whether it is time to reveal and share its power to others.

The original black box paper weight and a summary of the principles of one half of the book have already been revealed to the world decades ago. On its own it cannot sustain its power, the black box teachings and focus of achieving material power will only bring temporary benefit to the privileged few. In the coming decades you will see evidence of the principles, it will be written about it will be the foundation of many enterprises, economies, religious movements and societies. But eventually these principles will not achieve their true purpose without the secrets of the white ball and the principles of creative power.

The Black Box principles will eventually lose power and momentum until they are united with the *'white ball principles'*. The Black Box Principles will for a few privileged individuals teach them how to master the six sides of the Black Box;

I. The Leverage of others labour and skills. (Human Resources)

II. The Creation of a definite plan & purpose. (Management)

III. Serving others with specialised knowledge or skills. (Products or Services)

IV. Persistence and the understanding of human desires and fears. (Sales)

V. Material wealth through the mastery of financial education (Finance)

VI. The power and orchestration of organised systems, processes & people. (Operations)

The mastery of which has given our family wealth and success. Unfortunately this alone may provide *'material'* power for several decades or even a century, but eventually this will not be enough to secure a nation, its government, social or religions economic superiority or power without the 6 secret characteristics of the White Ball.

The White Ball is about the 6 characteristics of creativity;

I. The Spirit; Passion.

II. The Believer; Faith.

III. The Inventor; Ideas.

IV. The Designer; Vision.

V. The Gambler; Risk.

VI. The Rebel; Courage

I entrust this in your safe keeping and only wish that it brings you wisdom and happiness".

Chapter 2

The Worlds Creativity Park 2061, Glasgow

A gentle vibration from my I-watch startled me briefly and awoke me from my daydream indicating a message from my I-assistant, old habits die hard I still couldn't give up this one piece of old technology. A soft gentle voice could be heard from my audio fashioned hear-ring chip "You will be arriving shortly at your destination, the south gate of the Worlds Creativity Park, your two guest passes have been registered to your identity chip to allow you immediate access, and your Grand daughter Annie has confirmed her arrival and will meet you at the main reception, you will arrive at your destination in approximately three minutes", a gentle beep indicated the end of the message, resuming e-hearing aid mode.

I gazed out of the window as I approached my destination in the distance was the city skyline with the back drop of a beautiful clear blue sky. The city landscape had changed over the past 50 years, that old damp and depressing grey image of dirty tower blocks, decaying buildings and ugly wind farms blotting the horizon had been replaced with an image of optimism.

This landscape was now filled with beautiful stretches of roaming gardens and greenery interspersed with scattered areas of small groupings of chameleon like Solar-mast windmills with their fine high-tech blades and colour changing technical textile masts opened and elevated in solar mode. Other than the A-listed buildings little remained of 2 or 3 story buildings, everything was now vanishing underground. Our landscape and way of life was now redefined by new feats of engineering and architecture. In the distance you could see the glass dome of the Creativity Park set in the large expansion of small grass covered undulating hills and Botanical gardens.

The skyline was gradually reclaiming what this country was renowned for, its beautiful natural landscapes and scenery and hothouse environments for inspiring the mind and soul. Its reputation was firmly intact as the worlds leading creators of innovators and visionaries of architecture and engineering, how my grand parents would have loved this, how things had changed. Some things had definitely changed for the better gone were the days of texting and rummaging about in your handbag for your i-phone, no more driving your electric car into the city, worrying if you had your credit card to pay for your out of town parking and having to take a monorail into the city, oh life was so much simpler. Already identity chips were almost obsolete and everyone was now using face recognition. What was the world coming to?

As the chain of vehicle-pods reached the entrance to the South gate the single occupant pod disconnected from the chain of pods and gently glided into hydro mode on its approach to the Worlds Creativity Park. The pod approached the door and aligned the door seals for disembarking, as the suction seals engaged I gave my pod navigator verbal instructions to self-park in the low level road bays and await instructions from my I-assistant when I would be ready to leave. Both the doors to The Creativity Centre and pod opened simultaneously and my seat slowly retracted out of the pod with the chair slowly adopting the upright standing position before disengaging me from the waist and shoulder safety supports. I slowly steadied my feet and waited momentarily as my intelligent clothing system re-configured, my wellness sensors adjusted the inflation in my shoes to reduce the pressure points in my feet to compliment the flooring, simultaneously my clothing fibres altered in temperature and colour with the change of environment and light. At 91 I still liked stylish clothes but fashion was now secondary to my wearable technology and its health & mobility benefits. I walked slowly ahead, only to be welcomed momentarily by the sound of Annie's warm voice.

"Hi Gran" with open arms & a wide smile Annie wrapped me tightly in a bear hug.

I never grew weary of that beaming smile, ever since she was a little girl she would light up every room she entered with her positive energy, comedy timing and unconscious wit. Still embracing we both looked at each other and giggled.

"Happy 17th Birthday, Honey" I said sincerely.

"Where's Granddad?" said Annie disappointedly.

"Oh! He's looking forward to seeing you, he's just meeting a group of kids he mentored last summer who are in town for the Sports Technology conference, and then he's going to meet us later for lunch" I said.

"Anyway I wanted you all to myself this morning, no interruptions" I said as I switched off my I-assistant and we both locked arms and slowly made our way through the identity-scanner to the main reception of the South gate, pacing myself as I went. The sound of music and a familiar voice met us as we approached our first ritual stop the virtual receptionist.

We both stopped and gazed at the life size female hologram fixed to one spot with a plaque at her feet with the inscription:

"Donated by the founders of Y.P.T 2020. With the unconditional love, patience and encouragement of parents, grandparents, teachers and guardians we can teach the spirit of 'creativity' and enable a generation to believe once again that they can become the worlds leading creators, innovators, thinkers and problem solvers."

As we stood the hologram began commentating on the lives and works of great entrepreneurs, innovators and creative minds-as the screen behind her changed through form and colour, from black & white to coloured film, to 3D film through to 5D Action with bursts of vaporising scents and smells.

"Welcome to 'The Worlds Creativity Park' we hope you will enjoy this interactive experience and celebration of the world's greatest creative minds from designers, innovators, to artists, film makers, thinkers, scientists, engineers, entrepreneurs and writers. Please open your mind to the power of 'Creativity' and enjoy being our guest as you celebrate the lives of those who have shaped our economy and society of the 20th & 21st century."

The holograms silhouette faded gradually in the light and then vanished before our eyes to the gentle sound of soothing classical music. Momentarily the sophisticated lighting system dulled as the entrance door and roof retracted to gradually reveal the vast 'Musk Dome' the solid solar powered hemisphere of glass from ceiling to floor was gradually flooded with the rays of bright natural sunlight to reveal the Creativity Centres circular atrium. Gradually the sunlight triggered the solar fibres in the carpet to change the appearance and colour of the carpet tiles from grey to yellow. Annie looked at me with a cheeky grin as we linked and locked arms laughing as we made a feeble attempt at a skip and a jump, giggling as we made our way across the floor of the atrium.

From the tender age of 5 this place had never ceased to inspire, teach and bring pleasure to Annie with the various interactive displays of creativity, imagination and innovation. As she grew older she gained a greater and deeper appreciation for the secrets hidden and revealed in the 6 low level underground walkways and tunnels that lead from the lower level of the circular atrium. The design and architecture were still inspiring even by today's standards, ideas taken from the great engineers and creators of the Hoover Dam and Euro Tunnel.

Annie turned to her Grand mother "Gran, it's fantastic my Y.P.T (Youth Pension Trust) has now been activated and I can choose between 4 years of volunteering, apprenticeship, entrepreneurship, travelling or university study….. I know that I want to set up my own business but I just need to find the right idea" blurted out Annie ecstatically.

"Well honey, we are in the best place in the world for a little inspiration" Gran said squeezing her arm affectionately.

As we strolled across the atrium I motioned to Annie to stop to have a momentary seat at one of the observation and group assembly stations. We watched as groups and parties of school children of all ages and nationalities flooded into the vast dome.

Grand parents and parents huddled together with their children and grand children as they excitedly made up their minds which exhibition to enter first, they each scanned the tour app on their flexible TV screens displayed and embedded on their sleeves. Many were wearing the latest craze in recycled wearable technology which uses the next generation of washable and wearable electronic fibres to create fabric structured electronics.

The sun shone through the dome radiating the atrium with sunlight and the atmosphere of a warm summer's morning. We gazed out of the Musk Dome across the Creativity Park s garden of beautifully trimmed lawns interspersed with local indigenous botanical displays of rock features and tall lush trees. The Solar-mast windmills slowly and inconspicuously in unison changed direction with the morning sun, altering in reflection and colour to blend with the surrounding landscape.

Inside the atrium you could clearly see the 5 legendary figures depicted as holograms welcoming visitors as they approached each of the elevators that carried visitors to the lower level atrium where visitors would begin their journey to their individual destinations in the West or East wings; The legendary inventor James Dyson, visionary Walt Disney, philanthropist Andrew Carnegie, Entrepreneurs Dame Anita Roddick and Sir Richard Branson.

"Annie I don't know if I have ever told you this but do you know what made every one of those individuals different to every one else of their generation?

"No Gran" replied Annie curiously.

"They were all risk takers, non-conformists, non-traditionalists, free thinkers, innovators, dreamers and rebels in their own way. When your mother was 5 years old we found ourselves as a Western civilisation in one of the most controversial ethical and economic periods in our history since the 1930's. We had a legacy of public and private companies including the banks which had kept working to business models, principles and solutions designed seven decades earlier that were no longer fit for purpose. We were part of a generation living on a staple of popular culture that told us we could have it all. Some people in power bought into the belief that they were above the law, were untouchable and could govern by a different set of values and rules than the rest of us; Politics, Media, Religion, Policing. We all got greedy maybe not to the extent of the banks, but we started believing in the illusion we were sold that we were entitled to a lifestyle of luxury homes, cars, gadgets, designer clothing & luxury holidays while our monthly expenses, in terms of mortgage and credit cards exceeded our monthly earnings with an economy that in the main no longer created or produced anything tangible.

The masses ignored the importance of financial education with the majority of us convincing ourselves that the gravy train wouldn't end. We adopted a lifestyle of wasteful consumption without care or consideration of the consequence of this new lifestyle and culture we were teaching our children, with its damaging effects on our environment and resources.

Our governments put all their eggs in one basket, namely big business and the service & financial industries. They neglected the back bone of our country, the small business and the source of all great research, development and innovation. Instead of reinventing our manufacturing industry we simply became a nation focused on big business self obsessed with advertising and marketing.

All the while our competitors had the foresight to invest in creative small business's the future and innovation. While other nations held onto their gold reserves and got financially educated we sold off all our national assets, manufacturing capabilities and gold. We went to work leaving our brains at home and some how thought we could still be world leaders.

Remarkably from the depths of a recession, disillusionment and frustration a spark of inspiration came from the combined efforts of the young and old, a new generation of young thinkers and a passionate group of old 1960's hippy's. They took inspiration from these great social entrepreneurs, pioneers and role models such as Robert Owen, Anita Roddick & Jamie Oliver. They realised that single enterprises and the individual could make a difference. They harnessed the strengths that big business couldn't compete on; individual passion, the speed and mobility to adapt, the ability to specialise, be innovative and have a social responsibility.

They created a new model of business a new way of thinking about business other than just profit. They created a business model and thinking that measured success in the gains and improvement to the community, environment, society, ethics and financial profitability. And with one single enterprise or micro business at a time began rebuilding our economy to reap the benefits of everything we see before us.

We sat momentarily as I regained my composure.

"Well enough of my ranting, where should we adventure to today, where will we start the West or East wing? It's the birthday girl's choice" I said.

"Lets start with the East Wing and visit the Inspirational Garden" said Annie firmly.

Chapter 3

Home

Mary and Duncan were now married, after a short ceremony a year ago scheduled at the last minute during Duncan's leave from the RAF. Mary now found herself all alone in what was now called home. Mary sat in the spare up-stair bedroom of her mother-in-laws house looking depressingly at the four brown soot stained walls. Mary was now expecting her first child but found herself depressed by the thought of how she would cope in the coming few months with a baby on the way being in a strange house with her husband hundreds of miles away and her Mother, brothers and sisters back in Ireland.

Sitting alone Mary sighed a sound of relief, finally she had a little time to herself to collect her thoughts as her mother-in-law and sister-in law set off for the day to visit an old aunt several miles away. At last a little peace and quiet, how she missed the peacefulness of the farm in Ireland and those long quiet walks with Duncan on the Keir House Estate.

Kneeling down on her bare wooden bedroom floor Mary reached under the bed and pulled out her small battered suitcase and placed it on the bed. She opened up her suitcase and began emptying one by one the few material possessions she owned in the world. The last thing left at the bottom of her suitcase was the gift she had inherited several months ago wrapped in brown paper and string. Between the commotions of the Clydebank bombings, the organising of their wedding and preparations for Duncan going off to War Mary hadn't had time to think about the book and the paper weight. As Mary sat on her bed unwrapping the gift she wondered if its contents would offer her and her baby some hope and answers for the future.

The book was covered in coarse heavy brown leather with thick hand bound stitching, on closer inspection the book was made up of two parts bound back to back, on one side the book had an embossed square box and on the other a circular globe. The writing although in a small old script text was readable. The thought of reading the manuscript didn't daunt Mary. As the eldest of 8 children aged only 10 when her father died leaving her mother a farmers widow in Donegal, Mary and her mother worked tirelessly to put each of her brothers and sisters through school. Mary was a confident reader having been taught the indelible cost and value of an education, and that books are the key to opening the potentials of our mind. Learning to count, read and write came at a cost; it was paid for by those long hours working in the fields with her mother and those cold wet autumn days spent pushing and shoving a donkey, knee deep in sodden wet peat, cutting and stacking the peat on

the side of the road to provide their families share of peat for the school house fire for keeping them warm in the winter.

Mary sat down on the wooden floor next to the fire with her back resting on the bed. Gently she placed the leather pouch on the fireplace hearth and then slowly opened the book. The pages of the book were thick and stiff and all firmly intact in the spine of the book, as she turned each page there was a gentle dusty aroma. The pages though almost tea stained and brown with age, were free of finger prints or creases like precious old photographs or drawings that had been carefully handled and cared for over time. For a few seconds Mary closed the book cover and held it tight to her chest pondering on what the contents of this book would reveal, as she hesitated she thought of that evening when she was surprisingly given this unusual gift.

Mary placed the book in her lap and slowly opened the embossed 'Black Box' facing side of the book. Immediately she noticed a piece of folded paper tucked in the books inside cover. As she gently removed the delicate piece of paper she realised on closer inspection that it was a letter.

The letter read:

Dear Entrusted,

I bestow this gift into your safe keeping and hope that it brings you the blessings and joys it has bestowed myself and my loved ones.

Before you begin this journey I ask that in return you simply commit to four basic principles and by doing so gain the full appreciation and benefit from the contents of this book that accompanies the two paper weights:

I. Read both manuscripts and the book in its entirety.

II. Commit to mastering the six elements of the white ball & black box.

III. Open your mind; be inquisitive, creative, questioning & develop your own thinking.

IV. Entrust its teachings in the spirit of your children.

The contents of this book will take you on a journey to discover two philosophies. Life and nature sustains itself through a natural balance of opposites. The teachings of the 'white ball' and 'black box' are two separate and very opposite philosophies which when combined can create genius.

The creative power of the White Ball will help you discover your spiritual purpose in life. The White ball is a free flowing moving object, bouncing, rolling and always in perpetual motion. Unlike the Black box which is static, rigid & fixed it thrives on freedom and movement like snow flakes in the wind. It is a powerful human centred philosophy. The personality of the white ball is very similar to the spirit of a child the youthful dreamer, the believer & the free thinker. The White Ball has six essential characteristics:

I. The Spirit; Passion

II. The Believer; Faith.

III. The Designer; Vision.

IV. The Inventor; Ideas.

V. The Gambler; Risk.

VI. The Rebel; Courage

The material power of the Black Box will help you discover your material purpose in life. The black box is a fixed stationary object with limited movement. It is a systems centred thinking focused on simplified order, clear disciplined roles, functions, plans and strategies. It derives its power and success from follower personalities who like order and rules and the need for conformity, conventionality and structure. Each side of the black box cannot function independently without influencing and impacting on each other side of the box. The Black Box has six basic functions:

I. Human Resources; leverage of others labour & skills.

II. Products or Services; serving others with specialised knowledge or skills.

III. Finance; material wealth through the mastery of financial education.

IV. Operations; the power & orchestration of organised systems, processes & people.

V. Sales; persistence & the understanding of human desires and fears.

VI. Management; The Creation of a definite plan & purpose.

I hope that within this book you will discover the wisdom and insight to fulfil your dreams.

Anonymous x

Mary sat for a moment and slowly digested the contents of the letter. She read the letter once more and then gently folded the letter close and placed it back firmly in the inside of the book.

Time passed quickly, and before Mary knew it she had given birth to a beautiful healthy son shortly followed with news of Duncan's posting in North Africa. The world seemed in an increasing state of turmoil most of all the young men were now away to War either stationed in England, mainland Europe or North Africa . All travel from mainland Britain was restricted with many Irish immigrants or visitors stranded in Britain unable to travel by sea. Everyone waited tentatively for any news of their sons, brothers and husbands with the arrival of the post master or a knock at the door.

Life in some ways was much simpler with everyone being more grateful and appreciative for the small things and simple pleasures like receiving a letter from a loved one or individual moments when the war was briefly forgotten about. Everyone had a deeper appreciation for the important things a family celebration or Friday night sing along with family, neighbours or friends. For all our worries and fears we lived in the moment and cherished the blessings we had of our children, family and friends. Mary took every opportunity to send photographs to Duncan of the son he had not yet met, attempting to capture and share those precious early images and moments of his childhood before they disappeared forever. Unsure of how long the war would last Mary attempted to ensure that their son wouldn't be a stranger to his father when he finally returned home.

Everyone's lives were now about simple needs with everything rationed from fabrics and clothing to sugar, dairy produce, fruit and vegetables and tined produce. The local auction houses were doing a roaring trade they had never been so busy trading in second hand furniture, carpets and clothes. Mary's enterprising spirit prompted her to take what savings she had to rent a small allotment to grow her own vegetables and buy a few chickens for laying eggs. She had learnt many skills from her time working at Keir house in the kitchen and from the many hours she spent working with her mother on the farm, from how to preserve and store fruit, vegetables, jams and pickles.

The months passed and before Mary knew it her sons first birthday past, and then his second birthday with no sign of an end to the War. On a cold winters evening Mary quietly made her way upstairs with her son, depressed by more radio reports of further bombings and casualties of the War. In her little bedroom she sat in her old wooden armchair with her son wrapped in a shawl. Mary sat reading her son to sleep with Duncan's letters and postcards before tucking him up in bed.

Tired but unable to sleep Mary stared at the fireplace full of melancholy and despair as to what the future would hold for both Duncan and her son. Slowly Mary knelt down on the carpet and reached under her bed for her old battered suitcase pulling out the brown leather book still wrapped in brown paper and string. With a large crochet shawl wrapped tightly around her shoulders Mary sat down in her chair and with a little trepidation opened the White Ball cover and began a night of reading.

Chapter 4

The Inverted Atrium

Annie and her grand mother along with twenty other excited parents, grand parents, teachers and children made their way to the large elevator door that would take them to the lower level and the Inverted Atrium before they reached the tunnel that led to the Inspirational Garden. We waited briefly as each of the six separate elevator doors, positioned around the edge of the atrium opened in unison to transport guests to their various destinations and gateways to a world of creativity.

We all slowly made our way into the circular elevator, with the doors closing gently behind us. It seemed almost instantaneous that the lights dimmed and the elevator doors reopened into deep darkness. The guests flooded out and dispersed one at a time along the wide open balcony that enclosed the rim of the large inverted atrium. As the last to exit the elevator we approached the balcony just as my personal audio fashioned hearing chip registered my presence. One couldn't hear a pin drop as the atrium began to fill with the resounding sound of a solo saxophonist.

Suddenly the inverted atrium transformed into a live cinema screen with the small image of a single flashing star lighting up the dark motionless atrium. Slowly it revealed the projection of a complex star system to the sound of the saxophonist. The sound of the saxophonist faded as the voice of an Angel called Clarence began talking to God about the life of a man called George Bailey as a deep black hole emerged from the centre of the atrium floor, transforming into a circular shaped film screen revealing an old black and white monochrome movie.

The movie began depicting the life story, character, values and motivations of this man George Bailey in hyper speed. As the man progressed through scenes in his life, fulfilling his spiritual and creative purpose, one good deed after another, the single star began to shine brighter and stronger. As each scene of the film unfolded and George touched someone's life instantaneously a new small star would appear connected to Georges 'star causing it to grow more magnificent and stronger. Simultaneously another instrument would join the sound of the solo saxophonist. Within a very short time the atrium floor was dazzling in spectacular colours with radiating stars of every colour of the rainbow accompanied with the sound of an impromptu orchestra performance. Eventually the screen of the film was hidden from view with the cascade of sparkling lights and stars, leaving us with nothing but the sound of this magnificent orchestra and the voice of the narrator the Angel Clarence.

As George's life progressed he faced new and more difficult challenges becoming increasingly despondent, confused and disillusioned. Then as if from nowhere faraway in the distance we could hear the despondent and distressed voice of George. Suddenly we could hear him uttering seven little words which rebounded off the floor of the atrium and across the vast room:

"I wish I had never been born."

Simultaneously as the words were uttered the whole atrium was turned into darkness and the room was now in complete silence. As we stood we couldn't hear a pin drop. Then briefly from the depth of darkness a single voice emerged and said:

"Life is Wonderful and ever changing in cycles of both fortune and misfortune, our ability to work through misfortune comes from the strength of our spirits purpose."

And then instantly a single saxophonist began playing again as a small star emerged from the darkness and began shining once more.

Gradually the lights were slightly raised along the balcony to reveal individual transparent computer screens placed strategically along the balcony edge. Each computer instantaneously invited each guest to contribute openly or anonymously to the 'Gratitude Book' sharing either the names or short notes or stories about individuals that had made a positive connection and influence in their lives from; teachers, parents, grandparents, mentors, brothers, sisters, colleagues to acquaintances.

As children and adults accessed their computer screens and began anonymously posting their notes of gratitude. One by one a new instrument accompanied the saxophonist and a new star emerged on the atrium floor. We watched as stars emerged and flashed across the inverted atrium floor. Within a few minutes the room was filled with the resounding sound of a philharmonic orchestra and the atrium floor was once more in full spectacular light and colour.

With a little sparkle in their eyes and a gentle smile on their faces children, parents, grand parents and teachers stood transfixed to the spot, gazing reflectively across the sea of stars inspiring everyone with 'A little soup for their souls'.

Silently Annie and I quietly turned and arm in arm made our way to the tunnel that would lead us to the Inspirational Garden.

Chapter 5

The White Ball: Introduction

One must always remember that the 'White Ball' manuscript is a human centred thinking rather than systems centred thinking, it represents six separate but interlinked characteristics and principles that have been taught and passed down from one generation to the next by the great creative thinkers, inventors and visionaries. One must remember that each characteristic has its own essential place and purpose in obtaining creative power. The six key characteristics of the white ball are:

I. The Spirit; Passion

II. The Believer; Faith.

III. The Designer; Vision.

IV. The Inventor; Ideas.

V. The Gambler; Risk.

VI. The Rebel; Courage.

The white ball philosophy is a powerful human centred thinking like a ball it is free, rolling, bouncing always in perpetual motion it has no boundaries, limitations or rules. White ball thinking is opposite to black box thinking its components are chaotic and random. It gains power and produces results through individuality, lateral thinking, undisciplined roles & thinking appealing to leaders, revolutionaries and adventurous personalities.

The white ball characteristics are most passionately demonstrated in the belief, vision, tenacity, creativity and innovation of our youth or young enterprises. Unfortunately those youthful characteristics to gamble, take risks, and rebel against conventionality often diminish as we move into adult hood or as our enterprises grow and mature. Like most individuals and enterprises as we grow we build functions and rules around us to the point that the white ball diminishes and gradually disappears as they are consumed by the six walls of the black box.

Genius can be seen in those individuals and organisations that have been able to retain and protect their creative spirit. Rather than being consumed by the black box they have found a balance where the black box becomes the protective case and frame for the white ball, and the material functions support the human functions. When you perfectly combine a white ball and a black box you create a powerful, self sustaining and evolving energy. Ones 'creative' purpose is our highest and most powerful purpose. Our 'material' purpose is simply the vehicle and medium we use in life to most effectively serve, protect and fulfil our creative purpose.

Before you proceed please take note that the white ball strength can also be its greatest weakness. It lacks systems centred thinking which can make it void of structure, discipline, and order and can be threatened by extinction due to its lack of connection with the material and physical world.

Chapter 6

I. The Spirit: Inspiration

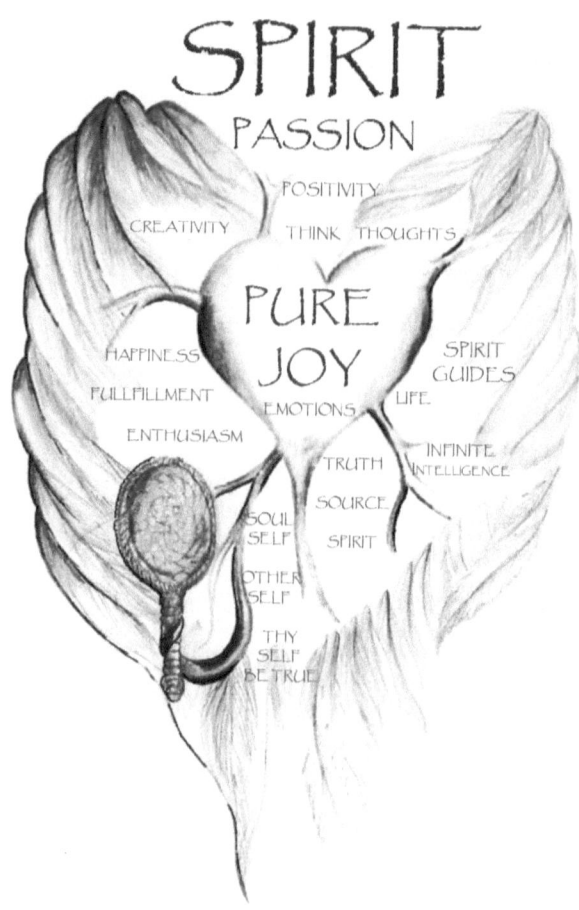

The source of all our 'Creative Power' begins with the spirit. The spirit has many names mother nature, god or infinite intelligence. We must learn to embrace, explore and understand this powerful intangible source of energy and inspiration. This is the essential tool that will help you connect with your individual creative purpose. Humanity is the embodiment of both our spiritual and physical self without this source of energy we would cease to exist. The first and most important of all the lessons in the manuscripts is this:

One must discover and find in life ones single 'Creative purpose'

Our 'creative purpose' is a definition of our highest and most natural values and when fulfilled demonstrate qualities of genius. To discover our creative purpose in life one must examine our self honestly. It often reveals itself in the expression of passion and enthusiasm when we are being most authentic, natural and true to ourselves in environments that allow us to express and resonate with our true values.

For those unacquainted to their creative purpose it often presents itself during our ultimate challenges in life or in that final defining moment of despair when we are at the point of giving up. Those restricted or limited by age, illness or disability often have a greater awareness of their creative purpose as they are often more highly tuned to their spiritual purpose rather than their material purpose in life.

Like wise it can express and reveal itself through our emotional frustration or anger when our creative purpose feels suppressed by others or by our environment or illuminated by an experience or event where it is demonstrated to be trivialised and undervalued. Unlike our material purpose our creative purpose isn't something we become, develop or work towards it is something we share as a gift unconditionally and freely with the world and humanity, often without the need of acknowledgement or reward. It is our spirits signature from the day we were born. Ultimately it is the gift we bring to others when we have nothing material left to share.

Ones ideas must resonate with our values

Everything we do stem's from honouring our creative purpose and being true to our values. When we do not honour our values we under perform and develop symptoms of procrastination, drifting, a lack of commitment or decisiveness. One must not be defined by past decisions and definitions of what or who we are, we must establish a foundation where individuals are not paralysed by their sex, age, race, creed, class or culture. It is paramount that there is a natural balance in all things and that the individual authentic female and male power, perspective and value are respected and honoured.

Once one has recognised ones creative purpose one must endeavour to focus and improve these qualities. Unlike the masses do not waste your time and energy trying to improve your weaknesses. One must honour our creative purpose before one can connect and tap into natures infinite resources. Only then will you draw and attract ideas to you effortlessly. Once we find our creative purpose we can begin the second part of our journey to seek inspiration for an idea to achieve our material purpose. Remember though an idea must connect and resonate with our true self for it to ever manifest into reality.

We must find our place of Natural solitude

To tap into ideas continually we must fully understand how to connect to infinite intelligence and our spirit and then define the environment and tools that best serve our individual needs. As humans our closest and most direct connection to infinite intelligence is through nature and places of solitude void of man made objects or interference.

We are all closely surrounded by an abundance of nature from our gardens, parks, lakes, loch sides to mountains or beaches. One should seek places void of human contact that connect with Mother Nature and offer solitude, quietness and stillness or the sounds, touch and scents of nature or wildlife from sea life, wildlife, plants, vegetation, animals to birds. Each of us need to find our own place free of noise, interference, pollution or negativity whether it is in the traditional quiet place of worship, prayer or meditation where one can find peace, solitude and reflection i.e. the mosque, church or synagogue or in a silent corner of our home or garden. Alternatively you can create your own place of natural reflection by simply finding a place that is quite, void of man made objects and then surround your space with strong sources of natural energy i.e. precious stones, plants or water features. Once we have found our place of solitude we can begin to use our tools to connect with our spirit.

We must choose our individual spiritual tools

To help us on our journey we must discover the tools which resonate with us most. One tool we can choose from is the 'spirit guide'. Depending on your culture or interpretation of faith a spirit guide could be, a prophet, spiritual leader deceased loved one or simply a living source of inspiration. It is someone who can help guide and connect you to your spirit & infinite intelligence.

If you decide to use a spirit guide it should be someone whom symbolises a source of love and resonates with your values and principles. You can call on their essence of spirit for support during the stillness of meditation or prayer. And can be an internal friend and inspiration to share thoughts, feelings and ideas with during periods of reflection.

Detachment tools

Individual's who find relaxing a challenge, may find using a 'detachment tool' such as humour or laughter as a great means to breaking the emotional patterns of an exhausted mind. By distracting our mind with humour, laughter, dancing, singing or even crying one can abruptly break a link with old patterns of negative behaviour. Like wise physical activity has always been an excellent tool for motivating a change in energy or clearing out of negative forces or ailments. As humans our emotions are intrinsically linked to our brains. Therefore by stimulating our emotions we can change our current pattern of thinking and behaviour creating an opportunity to clear our mind from old debris making way for a new focus.

Likewise inspiration often comes to the relaxed and still mind during sleep, daydreaming or the awakening from a deep nights sleep. Many of humanities achievements have been conceived away from the place of work and study in restful environments during seasonal holidays free of stress, motion or action. Other positive influences include leisurely activities and relaxing pursuits i.e. reading, art, music or gentle exercise.

Positive Energy

The most essential tool to make the white ball succeed is 'Positivity'. Everything and everyone that surrounds us has the will to resonate with the forces of either negativity or positivity. The universe is made up of these two energy forces which are entwined in everything we see feel and touch. It is essential that you surround yourself with positive individuals and associates. Reflect seriously on the influence of both positive and negative personalities and characters you regularly share time with.

If one practices the art of meditation and prayer one should develop the skill of being able to clear emotional or spiritual blocks and forms of negativity that stop the flow of ideas. Find the resources and thinking to clear your mind of all negative associations and attempt to retain as positive a vibration as possible. Begin with short periods of focus until one can gradually build up large periods of time focusing on positive ideas, feelings and emotions.

With your own place of solitude and your choice of spiritual tools you can begin the second part of your journey to seek inspiration for an 'idea'. This can best be achieved by the practice of stillness, meditation or prayer. Through the art of meditation or prayer one has the ability to efficiently form ones own ideas in a relaxed and focused environment. And find inspiration to a single question through the habits of a clear mind and introspection.

Be inspired

We all need stimulating sources of inspiration that can capture our imaginations and inspire our souls with real life experiences and understanding of both failure and success. Many great achievers have been inspired to greatness through the shared experiences and real life stories of their childhood idols their parents, grandparents or role models. There is nothing more motivating and inspiring to a child's mind than the ingrained emotional experience of watching a loved one demonstrate their unconditional love for them through enduring sacrifice, hardship and struggle. Many of our greatest achievers have been motivated to great heights by the enduring love of a loved one. Even the most uninspired of souls can find their own source of inspiration in life whether you seek your inspiration from the history books and libraries or the real life stories of our individual ancestors, adventurers and pioneers.

Summary

I. *One must discover and find in life ones single 'Creative purpose'*

II. *Ones ideas must resonate with our values*

III. *We must find our place of Natural solitude*

IV. *We must find our individual spiritual tools*

V. *Detachment tools*

VI. *Positive Energy*

VII. *Be inspired*

Chapter 7

The Inspiration Garden

We walked down the large tunnel towards the exit for the gardens. Stopping momentarily as Annie locked arms with me while we carefully deactivated all our electronic devices. We were now entering the peaceful and technology free zone of the East wing no more interruptions, impromptu sounds of music, gadgets or communication devices. We were entering what I called my Valhalla my favourite location within the Creativity Park. This is where I felt most relaxed and inspired in the quietness, peace and solitude of my native countryside and the great outdoors.

As we approached Annie asked "Gran, I have always meant to ask, why is this destination in the park without a hologram of a great inventor, pioneer, rebel, entrepreneur or visionary?"

"Well that's simple Annie 'Nature or God' is responsible for the Inspiration Garden. So it needs no introductions, it represents a part of every one of us, who and what we are. It has existed and evolved on its own since the beginning of time. Nature is the purest source of truth and the most powerful environment to connect with 'infinite intelligence or our spirit' I have always found its stillness to be the most powerful of all inspirational tools.

The morning sun illuminated the exit of the tunnel. As we approached the exit we could smell the scent of fresh cut grass and could hear the gentle sound of twittering birds welcoming us to the garden. Immediately like natural triggers my surroundings opened the flood gates of my senses allowing all my childhood memories to come flooding back. Faintly in the background we could hear the sound of children playing and far off in the distance the faint gentle humming of the hydro trains.

We stood at the entrance of the tunnel and looked out across the expansive gardens with its natural man made Loch. It was remarkable the transformation of this landscape which was previously renowned and associated with the great industrial revolution historically a dirty and noisy hub of steel works, coal mining and ship building. The transformation in landscape and natural beauty was remarkable. Now environmentally re-engineered, this city captured the tranquil spirit and essence of our true native countryside and natural habitat which inspired an environment for deep reflection, meditation and relaxation.

The garden paths glided gently down the hill to small clustered areas of rock formations, water features, shrubbery and landscaped trees. The landscape was a blend of natural colours from the deep dark greens of the conifers, spruces and oaks to the strong colours of our native purple, pink and white heathers. The park was dispersed with small inspirational areas of colour, sound, movement and touch positioned sparingly around the perimeter of the small Loch. To the right of the park stood the East wing "Library" in all its grandeur.

Slowly the tensions in my shoulders subsided as my pace of walking slowed to a snail's pace with every one of my senses heightened in awareness as my body slowly detoxed from all the technological interference. Gradually every bone and muscle in my body relaxed as I took a deep intake of fresh Scottish air clearing my over active mind to one clear focused point of attention.

We slowly followed the pathways, passing the small snail shell shaped shelters where individuals sat in solitude snoozing or day dreaming, just enjoying the natural quietness of the park. Others walked silently in couples or enjoyed the park taking a gentle stroll or jog alone. Every so often you came across a father and son or grand father and granddaughter sitting close together as they fished quietly on the side of the Lochs bank or individuals lying under the shade of a tree daydreaming as they watched chasing white clouds. The silence momentarily interrupted by a small group of squawking ducks or the flapping wings of swans as they glided across the surface of the Loch before landing and splashing in the water.

The garden captured the elements of the natural Scottish terrain our great Highlands and Lochs with the springs cascading over the man made rock features and down the side of the hill from the raised glass atrium. While the breeze of the fresh Scottish air across the large expansive and unsheltered perimeter created the reality of the great open doors.

The park was filled with triggers of positive memories from my childhood and youth with small patched areas of wild berry bushes and crab apple trees reminding me of the adventures of in the countryside climbing trees and picking wild crab apples, strawberries, raspberries and gooseberries during our long school breaks.

Every so often you could see a small group or couple enjoy the beautiful summer morning practicing Yoga or Tai-chi in the peaceful surroundings of the Garden. The park offered a variety of different mediation spots from woven basket swings hanging from the oak trees, the snail shell shaped shelters to small shelters cut from the granite and rock features. Each spot had its own round granite plinth filled with sand, pebbles or shingle and a selection of meditation tools including weighted marbles, stainless steel tennis shape balls or empty sea shells.

We slowly passed a large rock face with an embedded chalk board listing this weeks late night events in the park; Friday star gazing, Saturday the national youth orchestra and Sunday a candle lit meditation evening. We finally stopped along the path and crossed the lawns to take a seat on a twin swing under a large shaded oak tree that looked out across the Loch. We giggled as we both repeatedly tried to steady the swing, after several attempts Annie finally steadied it and we both sat down together cuddling under the shade of the trees branches. I sat and closed my eyes as the gentle breeze brushed my skin and the warmth of the morning sun delicately touched my face while every bone and muscle in my body slowly glided into a deep relaxed trance.

Slowly the tensions in my muscles and bones relaxed and a slow and gradual surge of gold energy moved through my body down through my head gently sweeping away all the negative tensions. A gentle warm energy wrapping my shoulders gradually moved through my chest sweeping away all the negative debris, slowly encasing my back and then gliding over my hips down through my knees, ankles till it reached my toes. The fine speckles of negative tension dispersing through my veins and then out through my pours instantly vanishing into the bright sunny morning light.

I turned to Annie as she sat enjoying the silence and watched her bright gold aura dancing and sparkling in the sun, radiating with energy and life. The vibrancy of her smile and her youthful energy gleaming with positive energy as the little grey squirrels ran up the tree trunk next to her and the robins and finches gathered and whistled in the trees above us.

I sat there without all of my gadgets thinking of how easy it was to find clarity and focus with this stillness and silence. I sat looking at all this magnificence and for all of humanities sacrifices of labour in creating the wonders of technology, innovation and science how we had came full circle to realise that there were certain things we couldn't replicate or perfect and what nature had already given us many of our answers and solutions for free.

This was always the best part of the Park to visit first, it immediately encouraged you to find a focus or purpose to the day and set your magnetism to resonate in a positive vibration and energy to prepare you before you ventured into the other destinations in the park. This closeness with nature always energised my intuition and my instincts and like the great library perched on the highest point of the East wing garden I felt my feet grounding into the earth with Mother Nature and my energy extending out and up to the bright blue heavens.

We sat without awareness of the passing time with the many park guests synchronised with nature and the great outdoors either day dreaming, meditating, praying, healing or relaxing.

Chapter 8

II. The Believer: Faith

Hand in hand with the *Spirit* is the *Believer* it is only with belief, faith and self belief that anything can ever be achieved. Some of us have been bestowed with this natural attribute of faith which is often formed by our individual upbringing or early experiences. For the rest of us it is a quality that must be diligently practiced and mastered. To truly create anything noteworthy or unique we must begin with the capacity to believe in possibilities;

One must be willing to believe anything is possible

Ultimately you must believe before you can conceive or achieve anything. For anything new to exist you must have faith & confidence in what others have not yet thought possible. It is a quality easily accepted by children but often the greatest challenge to adults. Through out history individuals of great achievement have either inherited or mastered this skill. They have inherited their faith through a higher source, nurtured self confidence, education or practiced skill. Some have mastered belief through conquering a great fear and obstacle, others from a deep seated self determination to succeed motivated by a great love or inspired hero or heroine. Ultimately everything starts with the power of ones emotional experiences and references in life.

Self Belief

For those lacking in self belief one of the greatest examples of how to adopt self belief is through the example of our traditional religions. Amongst all faiths and denominations it is plainly understood that to instil faith one must capture an individual's early imagination. This is achieved with ancestral stories of inspiring figures of scripture and history motivated by the rewards of Heaven or the fear of Hell combined with the repeated rituals of prayer, the sacraments, liturgy and hymns. The same simple principles can be applied to develop the skill of faith. The more focus we give a thought or idea either through physical experience, practice or thinking the greater chance it will have to form into our belief system. And in turn will be easier for our brain to accept as new ideas, beliefs or concepts.

Surround yourself with believers

The most confident of individuals in life are those loved unconditionally and supported at an early age through success and failure by a loving parent, grand parent or mentor. For this same reason it is essential that you choose wisely your most intimate personal and professional friends their positivity or negativity, encouragement or discouragement will greatly influence and impact on your choices and beliefs. Even the most confident of individuals needs the reassurance and support of others. Well meaning friends with limiting aspirations and thinking will not support your self belief but hinder your momentum and quash your optimism.

Test your beliefs

Life is a journey of memorable experiences both good and bad of success and failure. The greatest test of what we believe cannot always be taught through lessons but more valuably through testing those beliefs in real life. One should not be afraid to test our beliefs and make mistakes, this is how we truly learn and grow. The greatest approach to conquering our limitations is in facing them head on. Through both personal success and failure we can at least form our own indelible beliefs. Every master of history will testify that no one has ever achieved anything noteworthy without first experiencing numerous lessons of temporary failure or defeat.

Affirmations

For those who sense a lack of faith or self belief one must begin with the tools of self suggestion through a simple positive question that commits intention and asks the brain to provide the solution to achieving a single objective.

I. Set a goal as a positive question in written words related to what you wish to achieve.

II. Commit to its achievement by a set date, in the present tense, signed by your self i.e. Why have I achieved my goal? …Why have I achieved great success …… by the day, month and year? Signed by you.

III. You must then be willing to use repetition verbally repeating your affirmation & visually replaying your intended outcome & objective in your mind daily.

IV. Allowing your mind to perfect your idea and plan as it progresses over time with the answers and solutions your brain provides.

If your belief is weak you can keep using autosuggestion to strengthen your feelings and thinking. This can be physically reinforced by using what means are at your disposal to strengthen your physical, mental and suggestive beliefs i.e. studying, books, mentoring, adopting new skills fulfilling new life experiences. Ultimately everyone has the capacity to master their own thoughts and develop their own beliefs through focused repetition and practice.

Summary

I. One must be willing to believe anything is possible

II. Self Belief

III. Surround yourself with believers

IV. Test your beliefs

V. Affirmations

Chapter 9

The Library

After our rest we began walking along the pathway that led to 'The Library'. The library was designed like a giant sculpted oak tree supporting two floors encased with etched solar-glass walls and a roof of gnarled sculpted branches which stood on the highest viewing point of the East wing garden.

"Gran I think its time for a cuppa and a wee scone" said Annie.

"That's just what the Doctor ordered" I replied as we made our way towards the library.

The library was a daring example of architecture, engineering and sculpture, combining nature and the latest in man-made technology. The internal structure and support of the building was carved like a tree from reclaimed oak entwined with a wide wooden spiral staircase with two suspended wooden floors. The library emerged from the ground and surrounding hillside like the outstretched hand and arm of Mother Nature reaching for the heavens with large external granite roots that branched out into the garden in every direction like giant tentacles. Its roots and foundations all carefully sculpted from the granite excavated from the park during the mining of the tunnels for the Creativity centre.

As we approached along the path that led to the library the solar-glass trunk encasement revealed a glass doorway which slid open automatically. As we entered the library we were welcomed by beautiful examples of handcrafted Art Deco wooden furniture, fixtures and fittings. The library floor was covered wall to wall with a stunning patchwork of various reclaimed woods that swept and encircled the giant oak trunk mimicking the internal layers of a tree trunk.

Each floor and level of the library was filled with a sea of high back chesterfield chairs upholstered in every Scottish clan tartan you could think of. The chairs were interspersed with clusters of tall wooden shelved circular pillars containing rows upon rows of old fashioned hardback books. With the combination of clever engineering and carpentry the tall pillars slowly rotated and moved up and down like enlarged engine pistons when you gently rotated a pillar or leveraged your weight on a shelf in either direction. Each pillar clearly marked with a vertical Celtic engraving; fiction, non-fiction, art, business, music, children's literature, poetry, mathematics, science etc.

The shelves were lined with books of poetry, literature, fiction, non-fiction biographies and autobiographies from; William Shakespeare, Charles Dickens, Robert Burns to Napoleon Hill, Andrew Carnegie, Dame Anita Roddick, Elon Musk, Walt Disney, James Dyson, Steve Jobs, Sam Walton, W. Edwards Deming, Michael E Gerber, W Clement Stone, Seth Godin to Robert Kiosaki. Expanding to subjects i.e. Personal Development and Creative Thinking; Norman Vincent Peale, James Redfield, Jack Canfield, Dr Wayne W Dyer, Anthony Robbins, Paulo Coelho, Malcolm Gladwell, Edward de Bono to Tony Buzan the list was endless.

We made our way through the sea of chairs, towards the centre of the vast room to the giant trunk that encased the elevator and made our way to the second floor and the 'Skibo Tea room'.

On entering the second floor we passed through the children's reading section where we were welcomed with the scene of dozens of children selecting books of J.K. Rowling to Roald Dahl from the pillared shelves and running off to find an empty reading spot amongst hundreds of gel bags decorated as wildlife characters. How odd it was to see dozens of children inspired and motivated in a technology free zone quietly wading through the shelves of old books literary works, fiction and non-fiction. I stopped and paused for a moment and reflected on how important it was to fill these young minds with faith in their own aspirations, thoughts and ideas. These young minds were the key to our future.

As we approached the doorway to the Tea room we could hear the gentle pitter-patter of rain drumming on the glass roof with a fresh mid morning shower, as the city sky became overcast with clouds. A greeter welcomed us and took our order before seeing us to a table and two slender high back Charles Rennie Mackintosh chairs that looked out across the East wing gardens. We sat while our greeter brought us a pot of tea in an old fashioned china tea pot with cups, saucers and silver ware and a plate of freshly baked scones.

"Annie, do you know what I love about books, it is one of the few mediums where the speaker can express ones thoughts, ideas imagination and share it with others infinitely in time. The greatest contradiction of my generation was that during the great drive for more technological communication we systematically destroyed the fundamental gift to communicate and listen to each other. Many of us lost a wealth of knowledge and expertise from our elders due to our misplaced priorities, busy life styles and an ignorance of how to stop to take time to talk and listen to one another. Technological communication artificially fed the void of people's loneliness and need to be acknowledged resulting in a generation consumed by social media. Dame Anita Roddick founder of The Body Shop said many years ago "the greatest sickness in our society is loneliness and if anyone of us has a product or a store that counteracts loneliness we will have a business that will last forever". Books are often humanities way of reaching out to the world to be heard without interruption to share a new perspective, idea or thinking. For me the books that fill this library represent an insight to great minds that I never had the great fortune to meet in life, but through their words they gave me some personal wisdom to achieve a deeper faith in my own ideas."

As always Annie sat listening carefully to my words.

"Talking about ideas Annie" I said attentively.

"My idea Gran, Yes I've thought long and hard about it you know I have always wanted to be my own boss and create my own business where I can be myself and play by my rules", said Annie.

"Yes" I said smiling.

"I just need to hit on the right idea I need something that I am passionate about, that I can believe in like you, grandad and your father."

Annie was very fortunate in that she had a great balance of both self esteem and self confidence, she felt valued for just being her while feeling very capable in her abilities and skills. From her practical life experiences she had a firm belief that there wasn't anything she couldn't master or conquer with a little time, thought and effort. Similarly she had a natural positive disposition and limitless belief of what was possible from her life references and experiences and positive sphere of influence of encouraging and supporting family and friends.

"Well here's a starting place. Every book I have ever read has formed, expanded or challenged my thinking. For me metaphorically these books became like the legs under this table and my dreams and ideas were my table top. Every time I read a new book I placed another leg under my table top strengthening my vision, conviction and beliefs. They reinforced what my instincts and intuition already told me about business and creativity. It has been an essential tool to the foundations of my thinking, expertise and knowledge and helped reinforce my confidence in my purpose. This building is dedicated to the spirit of 'Andra' a great entrepreneur, visionary and philanthropist whom understood the great gift of books, his material purpose and later in life his creative purpose."

"The only advice I can give you is first find something that is true to your heart & spirit, and true to your values. Whatever your idea is it must resonate and allow you to express your true nature, personality and character. Then focus on your strengths, skills, interests and build on them. The more you repeat a skill the more skilled you'll become, do not to be afraid to make mistakes if you don't make mistakes you can't learn or grow. If you have an idea that you believe in use this library and any tools at your disposal to build your confidence to attaining it."

These shelves are filled with experiences that shaped the lives and beliefs of great characters. Many were motivated by the hardship and sacrifice of their parents and ancestors. Others found motivation in the stories of their heroes and heroines or the love or loss of a great love. Some simply had the need to create a better life for themselves in the pursuit to make a difference. But every single one of them deep down had the drive to fulfil their own powerful Dream or *"The wish their heart made"*.

Chapter 10

III. The Designer: Vision

As mentioned before white ball thinking is a powerful 'human' centred rather than 'systems' centred thinking. A ball is always free, bouncing, rolling always moving in perpetual motion unlike the box which is static, rigid & fixed. White ball thinking is the polar opposite to black box thinking its components are like the designer and the visionary they are free flowing, chaotic and random they have a passion that gives them the energy to fire about like fire flies.

The Designer is the great visionary and dreamer. Many individuals first labelled as fantasists and dreamers finally obtain the title of remarkable visionaries, inventors and thinkers. It is our visionaries that motivate people and thus steer society's path into the future. Credible visionaries can paint pictures and images in the minds of others like great story tellers. They hypnotise and motivate their audiences like the great illusionists sewing seeds in their minds with ideas of what could be possible.

The visionary unlike the inventor needs an even greater sense of self belief and conviction for their ideas because they often have to share their vision with the world, the critics and non believers before it is ever a reality. The visionary has an impenetrable thick skin that allows them to dismiss and reject criticism and ridicule. They are masters of their emotions and are rarely thwarted by negativity or public rejection. They have the skill to mesmerise others with their visions and dreams making their follower's believers and contributors in a great and shared vision.

Without the designer we have no vision no final destination, plan, purpose or direction.

The skill to Visualise

The skill of 'visualisation' comes before the formation of any great 'vision'. Visualisation is the essential skill of the designer, a skill that can be embraced by everyone. The more powerful and detailed we make our visualisations the more powerful we can make our realities. Through out history every inventor, visionary, pioneer or entrepreneur possessed within them the skill to vividly picture their idea in their minds eye before it was ever translated onto paper or developed into reality. Creative visualisation is a magical skill that can positively manipulate our beliefs and our brains thinking.

We all have within us the resources to create images in our own imagination whether from the resources of our visual daily references, recorded memories or the influences of others drawings, paintings or art. We simply need to give ourselves permission to be childlike again and have the freedom to be creative. Simply close your eyes and convert your thoughts into a blank canvas and begin the journey of painting or drawing your vision or idea. If we lack the experience of visualisation search and find the resources to stimulate your imagination whether from nature, travel, museums, and art galleries to new innovations. Any new visual stimulus will leverage your ability to think differently and more creatively.

Our Vision

"Ones vision must be the Design: the plan, the working drawing of our intensions." With the skill of visualisation we can then begin work on our Vision. Our Vision is equally if not more important than any verbal or written goal or affirmation because a vision or picture as the old adage says 'is worth a thousand words'. Depending on the content of an image or picture it can make hundreds of different connections to our emotions therefore connecting more directly with our conscious and subconscious mind. With a vision one can store a single image in ones mind that we can retrieve instantly. It has the power and emotion to communicate a thousand messages from the depiction of symbolism, representation and association while simultaneously creating impulses of emotion through colour, texture and personal association.

We must gather up all our resources and assemble a single visual depiction of that which we would describe in any affirmation or verbal goal. This may contain personal portraits of our associates, symbols of dates, single phrases or names. The choice of colour in vibrancy, contrast and intensity must reflect our intentions, emotions and vision.

Only then can one begin to add realism to our vision by developing our vision into a dream within our imagination. By allowing our imagination to take over and adding all our sensory skills of action, movement, sound, touch, taste and smell then we can add a new realism to our vision.

By placing ourselves within the dream and rein act our desired outcome and vision through our eyes our vision will become more tangible and real. With this in place we can use the faculties of our imagination to repeat, relive and reinforce our vision and consciousness during our day and our subconscious faculties while we sleep at night.

In our dreams our brain has greater difficulty to distinguish between fiction and reality. Consequently the brain will work efficiently and calmly to find ways of realising your vision into reality. Because the brain cannot distinguish between degrees of fiction, be confident and bold in your hopes and dreams. Make your vision an amazing objective of desire to inspire and motivate our senses and passions.

Redesign

The mind of the designer will first listen to their instinct and intuition before testing the practicality and logic of ones ideas. The designers mind is like a miniature Theatre of the mind where a performance is repeated endlessly ever changing in detail, story line and plot until it is eventually refined and polished. The designers mind never ceases until it finds perfection in realising their vision and dream.

Once fully satisfied they will then put pen to paper experimenting with every conceivable version of their idea or plan repeatedly drawing, sketching and remodelling. A real designer will become consumed in the perfection of ones idea and vision through revision, reengineering and redesign. The task of the designer is to be patient, persistent and never tire of finding better solutions. Only once one has eliminated all alternative conclusions will one rest.

Only once one puts pen to paper can the Designer fully share his vision and dream with others. It is essential that we find the tools and means to vividly translate the details of our vision onto paper. The execution of our vision will be determined by the accuracy of our ability to communicate our thoughts to our associates and followers. Remember "God is in the detail!"

The Maker

Once one has finished putting pen to paper we can then let the functions of the Maker take over the carpenter, the builder, the seamstress, the weaver. The greatest designers and visionaries are often apprenticing makers, inventors and the 'designer and maker or inventor' is often one and the same individual. We must never underestimate the crucial role and function of the maker as great inventions are not the conceptions of theorists but technicians. Without the understanding and practice of a craft we lose the source of all our ideas. Without our technicians we are lost.

Take heed, have the humility to respect the valuable role of your makers because without them we do not have tangible skills and foundations to be designers, visionaries and inventors. Learn from the arrogance of past generations *do not allow a single generation to lapse without protecting and maintaining the skills and expertise of your technicians.* It only needs the lapse of a single generation to destroy the inherited skills of centuries and the link to the next generation of technicians, designers, visionaries and inventors.

Strategy

Strategy is the last and final stage. It is necessary that we allow the creativity of the 'white ball' full freedom to explore its boundaries and potential before we ever begin to discuss strategy. Once we start talking about a strategy we begin the process of inviting 'black box' thinking and logic into our conversations and not creativity. Strategy must only enter our minds once we are fully satisfied with all our creative experiments and outcomes. If the mind is allowed to begin planning and strategising too early in the creative process we steal the energy of the white ball and its creative capacity too early, limiting our potential outcomes and success.

Summary

I. The skill to Visualise

II. Our vision

III. Dream

IV. Redesign

V. The Maker

VI. Strategy

Chapter 11

The Dream Room

We took a small detour and walked along the long underground tunnel towards the 'Dream Room' in the East wing which was dedicated to the memory of the visionary Walt Disney. We briefly passed through an identity scanner then entered the circular foyer with its rows of concealed vertical wooden panelled lockers digitally illuminated with our names listed right to left in alphabetical order. Simultaneously the locker doors slid open displaying what I traditionally would call a 'Onesy' in my length and size, velcroed flat against the locker door. The multicoloured onesy with enclosed soled feet was made of a fine waterproof and stain repellent breathable technical textile.

Immediately the children and adults placed their jackets, shoes and bags in the lockers giggling and laughing as they slid on their onesy. Instantly there was a change in atmosphere and everyone's conversation was more jovial and relaxed with many adults adopting a refreshing youthful or almost childlike demeanour. As we began making our way towards the Dream Room our locker doors gently closed and the large wooden Dream Room doors engraved with the words *'Be my guest'* slid open gently.

The Dream room was a 60 foot wide white washed amphitheatre embedded in the hillside, with a flat sloped sheer glass roof enclosing the full length of the building joining seamlessly with the hillside and its perfectly trimmed lawn. The Dream room faced out across the East wing with full views of the Library and Inspirational Garden. It fully captured the environment of the artist's studio with its wooden floors randomly sprayed and stained with paints and inks. The room was dispersed with mini white curved partitions strategically placed to create small artist's studios. Each partition supported a vertical automated paper dispenser the full height of each partition and was equipped with a mobile artist's station with every conceivable artist material you could think of from paint spray guns, coloured inks, chalks and acrylics to coloured pens, markers and pencils.

This was truly a place where you could explore the freedom of being a child again, act like a big kid make a mess experiment and express yourself, you didn't simply have permission to let your hair down it was a prerequisite. Everyone had their own private space and an enormous canvas to express their great big vision and dream. The high curved internal wall of the amphitheatre was decorated like a mosaic wall with vision boards of Tom Watson of IBM, sketches of Leonardo da Vinci, Walt Disney's story boards and plans of Disney World and the great parks which were only created many years after his death. The Vision boards were inscribed with their affirmations, doodles and notes.

As we all selected our own artist's studio and partition the greeter briefly introduced herself explaining that the purpose of the dream room was to allow us to have the real life experience and freedom of being 'a maker' creating our own images without the influence and restrictions of technology with its limiting manufactured images and software programmes. Here our children had an opportunity to both express their imagination with our depictions of colour, texture and form and have for many their first experience of being technicians without computer gadgetry and software doing all the thinking and creating. I turned to Annie and said "I think I'll sit this one out" pulling up a small artist stool beside her, like numerous occasions before Annie released the large paper dispenser and secured her canvas into position before carefully selecting her choice of artists materials.

Then the young female greeter began speaking once more:

"One of the century's greatest contributors in studying and understanding the human mind was Tony Buzan, for those of you who think they cannot draw or have no creative skills he said, "The reason why so many people assume that they are incapable of creating images is that, instead of understanding that the brain always succeeds through continued experimentation, they mistake initial failure for fundamental incapacity and as its true measure of their talent. They therefore leave to wither and die a mental skill which could have flourished naturally. Today we would like you to have the opportunity to create your own tangible 'Vision board' depicting your hopes and dreams. Tony Buzan also said that: *"We make use of a massive range of cortical skills (brain functions); colour, form, line, dimension, texture, visual rhythm and especially imagination 'To picture mentally'. Images are therefore often more evocative than word, more precise and potent in triggering a wide range of associations, thereby enhancing creative thinking and memory"*.

Please take this opportunity today to first and foremost have fun. We have a variety of drawing tools & materials to choose from to help you to begin to develop your vision board. The reason we like to use old traditional tools is simply that a 'picture is worth a thousand words'. Here we can begin with an impression, a sketch a doodle an idea created from simply taking pen to paper. This is the starting point of making your minds idea a reality.

Here you have your own artist studio with an abundance of paper and artist materials and the freedom to make a mess experiment, reengineer, redraw, redesign perfect your vision tinker until it is perfected."

"Have fun!" the greeter said.

Immediately a buzz of energy and movement erupted as children and parents alike began experimenting with their array of colourful and interesting artist's materials. Within a short lapse of time the room gradually came alive with rows upon rows of large scale colourful paintings in various textures, lines and images. With rows of children and adult figures dressed in multicoloured onesy's with their hands and faces covered in paint laughing and giggling and smiling from ear to ear.

Chapter 12

IV. The Inventor: Ideas

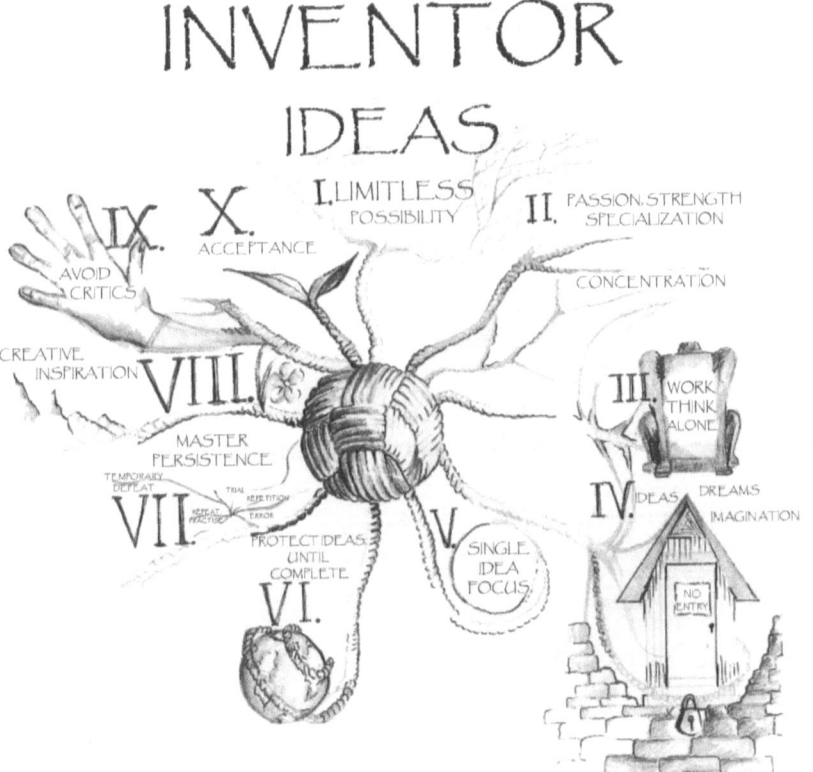

The role of 'The Inventor' creator or entrepreneur is the master of ideas. The inventor and their idea is the essential ingredient that makes each white ball unique. The inventor who celebrates their individuality and remains authentic to their values are those who have greatest ease in discovering their idea thus fulfilling their creative & material purpose in life. Additionally every inventor shares ten key principles that they work and live by which determines their success or failure.

The foundation of every great idea begins with these ten principles. The first principle is that which we have mentioned already it is essential that the inventor has the capacity to believe that anything is possible. Many of histories geniuses, inventors and revolutionaries were first described as simply mad, heretics, dreamers or fantasists. Throughout history the inventor has never been a character that has conformed to the days limiting beliefs or thinking. To be a true inventor it is essential that you unequivocally believe in possibilities.

I. Believe anything is possible

Without the capacity to believe the mind and brain will fail to generate solutions or ideas. The conscious mind of the inventor believes anything is possible and therefore when the mind is given a question as a statement with the expectation of a positive out come it will not rest until it produces a logical solution or answer.

The mind of the inventor is like a maze of coloured tangled wool with random brain waves shooting along each strand of wool in various random directions at hyper speed. Thoughts travel at the speed of light until they either come to an abrupt end when the thread of an idea instantly dies or finds a more viable route in another direction. The brain of the inventor is designed never to cease moving until it comes to a comprehendible solution. With the inventor there can be very a fine line between both genius and insanity. The mind of the inventor and their ideas are not unlike the white ball it loves the freedom to move, spin roll, bounce, and fly in any direction. The greater the power and force leveraged on an idea like the white ball the greater the momentum it will generate to break boundaries. For when the mind of the inventor receives a positively stated question their brain will not rest consciously or while the body sleeps until the brain provides the solution. The unconscious mind has no comprehension of limitations.

II. Focus only on your passion, strength and specialised knowledge

Every great inventor who has contributed anything of noteworthy value to life has had the foresight to follow their passion and focus their time and energy on their greatest god given talents and strengths. Only through the concentrated effort and focus on where you have greatest skill will you contribute something of significance. Anything of value doesn't start with mediocrity or weakness but inherent and natural aptitude and skill.

III. Work & think alone.

Solitude is the key that affords one greater concentration and focus to our own thinking. Alone one has the freedom of ones own decisions without interference of others opinions, thoughts and limitations. And therefore we develop the adaptive skills, resources and practical tools to explore our own train of thought and instincts. The need to predominantly work and think alone reflects the single mindedness and leadership inherent qualities in the inventor.

Any alternative means taking the risk that your ideas and thinking may be influenced and restricted by others limitations, values and dreams. And in reality what originally was your ideas and innovation simply becomes a diluted down version of your great idea and vision or at worst someone else's.

IV. Protect 'your' Inventors studio from reality and intruders.

Coupled with working and thinking alone is the need to protect your Inventors studio from reality and intruders. The Inventors studio or space is a sacred environment to every creative mind it is their place of solace and protection. It is like a mother's home or a banker's vault it is where one cares for ones most valued and treasured possessions.

It is the sacred place where one can shut the world outdoors and allow ones imagination to wonder into far off places of new ideas and possibilities. It is a place that must be apart from reality it's limiting beliefs and influences. Otherwise the creator cannot create and the inventor cannot invent and make progress.

V. Focus on one idea at a time.

To ever achieve anything of value we must concentrate our resources and focus on one single task at a time. By dividing your interests you simply slow your momentum and destroy your potential. It is important that you apply your efforts single mindedly to one idea at a time.

VI. Protect you idea from the world until it is complete.

The world is full of well meaning individuals and with ever individual comes a different set of ideas, opinions and beliefs. To fully protect the integrity of ones idea one should protect your ideas like the innocence of a child from the limiting beliefs and very real but often negative influences of life for as long as is possible. The longer our ideas are allowed to incubate and keep shelter from the glare and criticism of the world the more time we have to fully exercise our values, instincts and beliefs in creating the product of our mind and inspiration.

VII. Master Persistence

The single most important habit for every inventor is the habit of 'persistence'. Persistence is a quality that demonstrates hard work, commitment, self belief, vision and an unwillingness to accept failure. The ability to continue repeatedly and indefinitely to achieve ones goals demonstrates a stubbornness and single mindedness that is shared by great inventors, creators and entrepreneurs.

The finite detail and perfection of any great idea never arrives as an idea in its final form but normally in its raw and unperfected state. It is the tools and imagination of the inventor with persistence that refines, redefines and redesigns that idea again and again. With persistence the great inventor will perfect an idea internally in their mind as internal drawings, images, theories and designs. Until it is eventually ready to venture into reality onto paper and into writings, drawings or theories before taking its three dimensional form as models and then products. The value of any great innovation can often be determined by the level of time, energy and persistence any inventor affords their idea or innovation.

VIII. Find new experiences and sources of creative inspiration.

We all need new experiences and influence's to stimulate our creative faculties and thinking. Repeating the same routines, behaviour, thinking in the same surroundings will simply limit our potential perspective. It is essential that we retain the characteristic of the inventor of being inquisitive and adventurous finding new stimulus for our creative innovations and designs.

IX. Avoid the company of critics

The world is full of critics and experts. The negative and unconstructive critic is often an individual with resentments for their own unachieved ambitions. They would prefer to spend their lives decrying everyone else's dreams and aspirations rather than commit to pursuing any noteworthy idea of their own. Avoid the company of critics as their lack of aspiration and individual success will only frustrate and dowse the passion of the inventor or the entrepreneur. Our society is full of critics and can come in every guise from best friend, partner teacher to expert.

X. Acceptance

Be prepared when the moment comes to trust your intuition and instincts to accept when you have your 'idea'. Once one has that idea one must have the wisdom, conviction, intention and deep desire to begin the journey of making a plan and vision for putting that idea it into action. To achieve our 'purpose' we must now bring what we have learnt from these ten lessons and ask the inventor this question;

"Staying true to your authentic self and with your specialised skills and knowledge how can you provide a solution to humanities greatest hopes or fears?"

Summary

I. Believe anything is possible

II. Focus only on your passion, strength and specialised knowledge

III. Work & think alone.

IV. Protect your inventor's studio from reality and intruders.

V. Focus on one idea at a time.

VI. Protect you idea from the world until it is complete.

VII. Master Persistence

VIII. Find new experiences and sources of creative inspiration.

IX. Avoid the company of critics

X. Acceptance

XI. Staying true to your authentic self and with your specialised skills and knowledge how can you provide a solution to humanities greatest hopes or fears?

Chapter 13

The Designovation ® Studio

We exited the Dream Room through an underground passage way which lead to the underground tunnel to the West wing and the Designovation® Studio buried in the gentle undulating hills of the 'Creativity Park'. As our party lead into the tunnel, the light sensors detected our presence lighting the walkway before us while a narrator relived an interview with the great Steve Wozniak cofounder and partner of Apple.

"What do you think it takes to come up with a good invention? " **Interviewer.**

"You've got to have a pretty darn good idea in your head of an end goal. You can't just sit down and start using some tools you were taught and see where it takes you. You need one goal, and your goal has to coincide with something that somebody else wants to buy or something that will save them money." **Steve Wozniak.**

"One inventor I talked to said he never tells anyone what he's working on because people can be so negative. Have you ever felt that way?" **Interviewer.**

"Exactly, exactly! Right and left! Right and left! Right and left! And I put up with it. I'm really patient and nice to people. But it's hard when you have an idea and you want to implement it the way you see it and everyone else tells you why it won't work." **Steve Wozniak.**

"Do you usually work alone?" **Interviewer.**

"Anything that I've ever been proud of or was acknowledged for later was always done on my own. For example I wrote one set of code release for a custom microprocessor two summers ago when my wife was in Europe with the kids…..As it turned out during those three weeks were just enough time alone and away from the family, I got a ton of work done. I could go for a year trying to get done what I accomplished in those three weeks." **Steve Wozniak**

As the last of our party entered the arched Designovation® studio door way the lighting in the tunnel behind us dimmed.

Steve Wozniak continued "I knew I was going to be an engineer from day one….There's a certain window in your life when you're very young and you get a few things in your hands. And then, for the rest of your life, they're familiar and they're friends and that's your thing. If you got a car that you started working on in seventh grade, you'd probably be working on cars for the rest of your life."

We entered the circular Designovation® studio with its recycled hardwood floors and 180 degree curved glass window that protruded like a large fish bowl from the side of the hill. As we entered the studio the curved window slowly changed in colour from transparent to a fading grey tint, blocking the strong rays of the morning sun and dulling our view of the South wing gardens. The studio was designed like a small semicircle theatre, with what can only be described as oversized high gloss coloured snooker ball pods suspended from the ceiling facing the 180 degree window.

The curved walls were full of colourful children's paintings, prints and computer drawings of their favourite inventors, thinkers or visionaries, accompanied with their favourite quote or statement. One wall was dedicated to images of great Scottish inventors from Alexander Fleming whom discovered penicillin, Robert Watson Watt the inventor of effective radar, John Logie Baird inventor of the television, Alexander Graham Bell inventor of the telephone to James Watt the inventor of the steam engine.

A child's digital drawing of Thomas Edison read;
" *The first requisite for success is to apply your physical and mental energies to one problem incessantly without growing weary.* "

Next to a bright coloured painting of Alexander Graham Bell etched the quote:
"*Concentrate all your thoughts on the task at hand. The suns rays do not burn until brought to a focus.* "

The scooped out seat pods were dispersed randomly around the room carefully positioned along the four graduating floor levels and suspended a foot off the floor. On closer inspection each of the individual seat pods had their own transparent computer screen doors designed like retracting hoods that created the impression of solid balls. Quickly everyone made their way to one of the empty pods. The transparent hood doors retracted into the open position to allow everyone to take their individual seats, with only the smallest of children aged 5 or less doubling up with their parents or grandparents.

As everyone got comfortable in their individual pods the studio glass window turned into a vast transparent computer screen and a distinguished middle aged gentleman appeared in the centre of the screen dressed in an 'Creativity Parks' Technicians shirt. For foreign speaking visitors their audio fashioned hearing chips automatically activated to audio translation in their native language and for the hard of hearing the computer simulation of a young woman appeared on the right of the computer screen providing sign language and a written transcript of what was being said.

"Good morning everyone, my name is Anthony I am delighted to welcome you to our Designovation® studio, the place of Ideas. Here in our West wing we have a series of interactive rooms which embrace the latest advancements and inventions of technology. I hope that the tools we demonstrate today will give you the opportunity to explore your imagination and your creativity. First before I begin, please remember that our team have been lobbyists and leaders in protecting our social and human rights on personal data tracking. All data collected from our guests today will be automatically submitted to your private ID e-mail account as used when registering your park tickets and then disposed of from our records automatically. Many of our guests today are protected from 'personal data tracking' including those immediately protected under the age of 18", said the technician. "Our exploration today is to have fun exploring the depths of our creative potential and our imagination. As the great Albert Einstein said *"Imagination is everything. It is the preview of Life's coming attractions."* Everyone knows that the Designovation® studio aspires to our greatest explorers, our children in particular the spirit of those in the room under the age of 10 years old. But more importantly we want to inspire and motivate all you adults to expand your comfort zones and exercise some muscles you haven't used in a while your creativity, imagination and white ball thinking skills. If you are an adult and you feel awkward during these games today, let me reassure you, you are not alone. The Designovation studio tools are more challenging for adults to adopt because we naturally have more limiting beliefs ingrained from years of left brain thinking and our habits of socially conforming as adults. Our children have no limits to what is potential, their limitless imagination, thinking, opinions and boundaries of self expression are unrestricted simply by their lack of social conditioning. The Designovation® Studio is the room where 'ideas' are born, within the safety and security of your individual pods you can feel protected from the views, opinions and limiting beliefs of everyone else in the world outside. Within this room we have the freedom and opportunity to close ourselves off from the outside world to dream, imagine, hope and invent, in this place reality is an intruder. The Designovation® studio has been created specifically for those new to the creative process and has been designed to create an ideal environment for conceiving, nurturing and developing your own ideas.

Annie listened as she had dozens of times before with an expression of impatience on her face.

"History has proven that the life of a great creator begins with one great idea. In the past many creators conceived their ideas in an environment away from the world and all its distractions, in a place of retreat where one could silently create, imagine and innovate before sharing that idea or vision under the full glare and criticism of the world. Ideas conceived in the garden shed, the garage, the inventors and scientist's laboratory the musicians or artist's studio. Great ideas, inventions and products that define our future are triggered in those single moments of awoken sleep, that second dosing off in front of a warm open fire or that quiet solitary moment in the park. Each of our pods are one of many spaces in our Innovations park where one can switch off from reality and our lives and explore in a private place what we never imagined possible. For the next 30 minutes try and leave the limiting realities of life outside this room and open your mind and imagination. Today we are going to explore just a few techniques which I think you will enjoy using. Your individual pod computers have the vast resources of the internet with a library of images, data, facts, books, pod lectures combined with data on your individual profile. The Designovation® studio has been designed to maximise this creative experience and stimulate your senses during the creative process. For the adults I want you to imagine you are a young child again aged 5 or 6. Your grasp of the world has no rules, regulations, stereotypes, worries or limitations it is just a place of wonder opportunity, dreams, adventure and exploration. If you need a little inspiration why not take my designovation challenge and as yourself the question that we give to all our children". As Anthony spoke the question appeared on every ones individual screens.

"Staying true to your character & using your greatest talent, what would you create that would solve one of humanities greatest current hopes or fears."

As Anthony the technician spoke the temperature in each pod increased creating a more relaxed atmosphere and everyone's pods tilted backwards as the seats automatically moulded to their individual body shape as the room gradually filled with sunlight.

"I would like you to sit back and relax in your pod and begin your exploration into the world of creativity" said Anthony.

Everyone's computer glass hoods slowly retracted into a 90 degree closed position and then everyone's individual computer screens came alive. Annie began pondering the question and then excitedly activated the computer screen by touching it and authorising a transfer of her personal profile from her Private ID account.

Her Private ID Account enabled Annie to access both her aspirations and inspirational folders and library of books lectures and interviews of her favourite authors, inventors and mentors. Her inspirations folder contained her favourite music, art, personal images and catalogues of comedy's from; Robin Williams, Julie Walters, Rowan Atkinson, Jack

Black, Norman Wisdom, Billy Connolly to Peter Kay. Her aspirations folder combined her values & motivational profile, psychometric profile, leisure and creative pursuits, emotional interests and academic data (collated from her clothing & body monitoring which measures; heart level, body temperature, de-stress, concentration levels during practical, social and academic activities).

Once both folders were activated a margin appeared to the right of the screen providing a visual profile on Annie. A CTC brain scan image appeared on the top right corner of the margin highlighting Annie's Left and Right brain activity levels. And below a series of charts on her Values & motivations, Psychometric profile, Emotional profile, Academic strengths, Practical strengths, and People strengths. Her passions and skilled areas of interest were extremely apparent from the data collected from her heart rate levels during prolonged periods of time on single activities and the rated number of physical hours she spent on specific practical, social and academic subjects.

How did young people 40 years ago understand their individual potential without an education and curriculum designed and tailored around their individual practical, emotional, social and academic passions? How the world had changed with the re-engineering of our school system in terms of our social values and stereotyping about academia, practical and social skills.

Simultaneously the computer screen saver, the interior and exterior of the pod slowly changed to Annie's favourite colour blue and then a patchwork quilt of images filled the main central section of the computer screen. Annie's selection of synchronised inspirational music began playing in the background. The music continued to flow in Annie's favourite sequence influencing her mood to achieve alpha and theta brain wave levels for achieving a more creative and meditative state.

A patchwork quilt of images appeared in the central area of the screen rotating like an ever ending roll of cloth, rotating from one colourful, fun upbeat image to another from her library of images in her inspirations folder. At the foot of the page icons representing a row of old fashioned bound library books lined the footer of the computer screen with various titles: Annie's dream book and achievements book followed by favourite authors, comedians, inventors and personal development books.

As Annie placed her hand over a book, her bookmarked quotes and favourite comedy punch lines appeared across the patchwork of images. Within a few minutes the pod was a physical representation of Annie's motivators, influencers, interests and aspirations from the sound of the music, the temperature and colour of the pod, the panoramic computer screen visually depicted her passions and combined areas of interest.

Annie then selected her screen saver, her favourite meditation image and track embedded with the quote 'Imagination is everything 'a beautiful photograph and sound recording she had captured of 'Loch Lomond' on a bright summers day with the beautiful back drop of a deep blue sky accompanied with the sound recording of the water in the Loch brushing gently against the shingle beach and the gentle sound of a calm breeze hushing through the trees.

Within a matter of seconds the pod was set to her meditation profile and a series of Designovation tools appeared to the left margin of the screen, as Annie's heart monitor signalled an immediate reduction in her heart rate and stress levels. In the privacy of Annie's pod, she activated the Designovation® tools opening the mind mapping software a 4 dimensional wired ball.

Immediately a short demonstration showed how to place your frustration, goal or object in the centre of the 4 dimensional ball with clearly defined axis of North, South, East and West and Past and Future zones extending behind and in front of the central core of the ball. With mind mapping symbols and icons positioned to the right of the screen to trigger new directions, values, tenses along with a series of elaborate art and design tools. Immediately Annie placed an image and title that represented her idea into the centre of the ball and instantly began dragging her own coloured images, symbols and sketches into various positions of the 4 dimensional ball like a conductor conducting an orchestra.

She then took her false nail stylus from her pocket and with her index finger began sketching and adding numerous pathways and veins from her images exploring, random thoughts, impulses and ideas.

In what we thought was a passing few minutes was actually 30 minutes when the voice of 'Anthony' gently advised everyone that they had a few minutes left, before our creative session would end. And slowly the pods readjusted our seats into the upright position while the temperature dropped and awoke us from our hypnotic trance.

Chapter 14

V. The Gambler: Taking Risks

The role of 'The Gambler' is the risk taker, the adventurer and the explorer. The characteristic to gamble in life for fortune, ambition, love or truth is a skill of both courage and wisdom. Unfortunately no one has ever won or lost in love or war without first taking a gamble or risk. The term Gambler isn't isolated to taking risks with finances but taking calculated risks in life. We use the word 'gambler' carefully not in the context of recklessness or defiance without regard of consequence but with shrewdness and calculated intellect.

Taking risks is an essential characteristic of any leader or achiever. But equally it is one quality of the white ball which is greatly enhanced with the supporting structures of the black box. The thrill and emotions of risk can be both addictive and intoxicating and therefore must be mastered. The white ball characteristics are motivated by emotion and passion and therefore can find it challenging to reign in the emotional risks they are prepared to take. The spirited gambler is enthralled by adventure, competition, breaking boundaries and achieving what others dare not. It is a character of action, doing and daring.

Facing fear

The risk taker develops the skill of facing fear over time learning the difference between an irrational fear and a healthy fear. Powerful achievers develop the skill of rationalising difficult decisions through knowledge and facts decisions which to others may seem suicidal but which in reality are calculating and shrewd. The essence of the creative spirit is the need to push boundaries and limitations. The individualistic, self expressive and opinionated core of the creative personality is intrinsic to its rebellious nature. These human qualities are driven by emotion and passion which push the human spirit to their boundaries beyond fear, risk or ridicule.

Emotions connected to fear are often deep rooted in a lack of confidence or ignorance on a subject. Fear dissipates where knowledge, sound experiences and expertise exists. The wise risk taker will have a deep understanding of their area of expertise plus a sound financial education and understanding of the evolving world of finance.

Loss of wealth & respect

Human frailty is dogged by the fear of loss whether wealth, health, respect or position. The gambler best demonstrates and exorcises these fears on many levels and questions and challenges ones commitment and belief daily. The loss of wealth and respect is often the greatest danger of the gambler. But sometimes the painful experience of failure is the most powerful source of motivation. The education of loosing ones wealth, possessions, a loved one or ones respect can be the greatest of educations in building your defences and protecting your assets. Ultimate success often follows those whom have experienced the cutting blows and the bitter sweet pill of the descent from success to failure.

The painful experiences of loss or failure often force us to adopt the skills needed to avoid ever experiencing those emotions again. With experience shrewd risk takers develop emotional mastery and control of their decisions and impulses. Some believe that wealth is simply a transient form of energy which one must use as a tool. In this instance these thinkers protect and insure their own personal interests and simply trade new risks using others resources rather than their own or find the means of insuring and protecting themselves from any potential risk or failure.

Calculated Risk

Many who belong to historically wealthy families or achieve wealth of any proportion take limited or no personal risk. They accurately calculate risks often with the use of others collateral and resources as oppose to their own. To them the risk is often negligible and affordable in ratio to any potential gain. They are often diligent in saving their resources and preparing strategically for financial opportunities when the rest of the world is most vulnerable.

Certainty

The combining six characteristics of the white ball are all the emotional and spiritual elements demonstrated in various degrees of leadership. Taking risks is crucial to the white balls power and momentum. Leadership without risk is powerless and dying. A confident leader with certainty will have the will power and conviction to risk what is necessary to obtain their intended goal. What distinguishes the difference between a 'compulsive gambler' and a 'professional gambler' is instinct and intuition combined with 'certainty'.

Leaps of Faith

The creative personality resonates with the spirit willing to take leaps of faith. In adversity or strife the great leader when faced with a challenging decision will call on ones Spiritual guides for some divine intervention. The great benchmarks of history and defining moments are catalogued by men and women of history that along with their instinct and intuition and certainty were prepared to first take a leap of faith and making a full commitment to their decision before obtaining any guarantee of success.

Summary

I. Facing fear

II. Loss of wealth & respect

III. Calculated Risk

IV. Certainty

V. Leaps of faith

Chapter 15

The Great Pioneers

We made our way to the entrance of the last tunnel in the West wing where we were met by two greeters who helped us board our individual hydro-boards. Never in my wildest dreams as a child would I have imagined that instead of moving along with the aid of escalators or electric motorised chairs we would be fully mobile with water and static powered hovercrafts with retina navigation. It was bizarre being supported and transported in an upright standing position leaning on a metal skeleton spine that extended from a wheel free skateboard.

Side by side we entered the red paved hallway of fame, a long wide underground tunnel with large circular glass windows that looked out on either side to the West wing garden. The tunnel was interspersed with 8 protruding exploration pods which lined each side of the tunnel. Each pod offered workshops and interactive live skype discussions with international scientists, engineers, artists and entrepreneurs from all over the world.

As we glided along the hallway we were welcomed by life size holograms of 'Great Pioneers' lining the doorways of each exploration pod like a surreal image of the red carpet on Oscar's night. As we passed each hologram our personal audio fashioned hearing chips registered each individual commentary on each Great Pioneer.

The hallway was lined with the holographic silhouettes of individuals that had influenced and shaped our way of life James Dyson, Jamie Oliver, W. Edwards Deming, Elon Musk, Sir Richard Branson, Steve Jobs and Dame Anita Roddick. Our western economy and industries were transformed by these pioneers of space exploration, travel, innovation, engineering, energy, food processing and computing.

We stopped briefly and observed James Dyson's exploration pod providing a live workshop on engineering and design explaining the development and evolution of the 'Dyson' and his revolutionary engineering products. Then as we passed the hologram of my hero Walt Disney I reflected on a mans genius who inspired and motivated me in my childhood to draw through his animation but whom captured my entrepreneurial spirit and imagination as an adult through the genius of Disney World Florida. I stopped and paused for a second while my hearing chip briefly registered a conversation with the great man.

"I dream, I test my dreams against my beliefs, I dare to take risks, and I execute my vision to make those dreams come true. Dream, Believe, Dare, Do."

As I turned to move onto the next hologram I paused as a quote was recited from a book called "The Disney Way".

"The leader who dares to take risks is often an outsider who doesn't feel constricted by the establishments rules..... the French impressionist Claude Monet....was ridiculed by the art establishment. Walt Disney...as the producer of cartoons, he was looked upon as small time."

A small time cartoon producer whom with his brother Roy Disney had the vision and business acumen to achieve what any mere mortal would have believed impossible. The so called producer of cartoons, looked upon as small time purchased 29,500 acres of swamp land at $200 per acre in the 1950's which within 50 years would be valued at $1 million per acre for more than half of the land still unused.

Beyond the animation, film making and childhood animation characters was a visionary with financial intellect, operational mastery, engineering feats and innovation beyond just an animator. If only the rest of us could have just a little of that vision and genius.

As we hovered along the red carpet we watched as groups of children stopped to listen to re-engineered interviews or documentaries of past heroes. We stopped as a group of young girls stopped to listen to an interview with Sir Richard Branson.

I recalled fondly of being that age and the evening in my teens when my father came home from exhibiting at an Enterprise Show describing the euphoria that had been created from the arrival of this adventurous young man in a helicopter. He described how this spirited looking young character had captured everyone's attention and made his entrance dressed like the fictional character "Biggles" in jeans and a sheepskin pilot's jacket. I recall my father ending the story as he handed me a folded piece of paper saying:

"If my instincts are correct take care of this piece of paper because it might be worth something one day, and with it remember the lesson your Gran taught me, never judge a book by its cover, especially if they don't conform to your current thinking because there lies the first characteristic of a great Creative Pioneer. "

I watched attentively as the young girls were amazed at the stories and adventures of Sir Richard Branson and his various world records. They couldn't believe the stories of the man they knew as a great entrepreneur; his beating the fastest Atlantic Ocean crossing in a boat, his record for travelling from Dover to Calais in an amphibious vehicle. They were enthralled by the stories of his successful hot air balloon crossing of the Atlantic followed by his crossing of the Pacific from Japan to Artic Canada with speeds of 245 miles per hour, his attempts to circumnavigate the globe by balloon and an attempt of an Eastbound crossing of the Atlantic Ocean under sail.

By listening to his adventures alone it depicted the character of an inspiring by gone hero, adventurer and pioneer and invincible white ball thinker. But as the interview continued the young girls learnt about all his remarkable business's revealing a master of finance and economics with a sound financial education.

Beneath the stories was a passionate discerning character of vision that understood people's hopes and fears and a willingness to serve others and solve their frustrations. What may have been perceived by some as recklessness was the calculated risk of a good book keeper with the daring of a pioneering visionary.

Best of luck

We made our way through the hallway of pioneers reflecting on the potential power of one man or women's impact on society and our future way of life. This symbolised for me the greatest example of when white ball and black box thinking comes together. Without systems and order we cannot function as a society and without humanity and the creative human spirit we are soulless and stagnant.

These two historical characters defined what is our human potential, what would happen if we shared just a little of their courage to take a gamble and risk pursuing our Dreams.

Chapter 16

VI. The Rebel: Courage

The last characteristic of the "white ball" is 'The Rebel'. The rebel is the person whom has the courage to challenge our beliefs, our values and our thinking. Every progressive or developing country needs individuals who demonstrate and practice the courage to be different in every key function within our lives. The creative individual displays this characteristic with fervour from our poets, songwriter, activists, artists to writers their works are full of the fuelled passion of their words about truth, rebellion, politics and social injustice. To rebel, gamble & take risks are the qualities always demonstrated by the entrepreneur, the thinker and revolutionary.

Courage

Courage is summoned in the name of many causes the right to practice, exercise and protect our beliefs, our spirituality our right to love and be loved the sense and need of belonging of friends, family and community. Humanity is built on our courage to defend everyone's right of life and the basics of safety, food, shelter and good health. As society grows we need the courage to uphold everyone's aspiration to work, achieve and provide a contribution to society without discrimination against ones sex, age, social, ethnic or religious beliefs.

It is in ones questioning and defending of our basic values, ethics and our respect for our people, environment & community that the true human characteristic of the white ball is revealed. The energy of the white ball is powered by its connection to infinite intelligence as long as the white ball resonates with the courage and purpose for good and aligns with positive energy it will have an infinite source of energy and power. The character of the rebel is intrinsic to the life of the white ball it is its source of energy.

The new rebels and thinkers will very rarely come from the privileged classes and those of wealth. It will come from the fringes of society those motivated by their experience of being discriminated by their age, class, creed, sex and ethnicity. Like David and Goliath those sometimes quiet, unassuming and meek characters will be the next generation of young courageous men and women ready to change the world motivated by their experiences. Courage is not always about instant brut force but a slow strategy of shrewd and quiet intellect played patiently. If something is worth fighting for one will wait patiently. One will wait for the right moment using the same instrument of destruction and discrimination in reverse as an instrument and motivation for good.

Equality

Often having been the marginalised and judged one quickly learns the truth that all men and women are equal. One learns to never be mesmerised or manipulated by class, position, fame or wealth. From the experience of being dismissed, underestimated and discriminated ones intuition heightens and ones instincts sharpen to develop a keen sense of insincerity and falseness and an instant recognition of honesty and sincerity. The rebel will honour genuine friendships and associates and support their loyalty and friendship, likewise the rebel 'doesn't suffer fools gladly' and never forgets the names and faces of those that violate their values and trust. One learns to treat all men and women equally developing patience never to judge too quickly.

Breaking Rules

"Real creativity, the kind that is responsible for breakthrough changes in our society, always violates the rules. "Those most respected in history are those that have had the courage to ensure that their vision honours the spirit of the white ball and their love for their fellow human kind above the greed and self interest of the material black box. Qualities of the rebel are evident in the courage of our historical figures from Abraham Lincoln, Galileo, David Livingstone, and William Wallace to John Knox. Each one of them had the courage to break the rules and defend their beliefs rebelling against the conventional thinking and beliefs of the time.

To deny our thinking is to deny evolution and our will to progress as a society. The rebel embodies courage and self determination. Humanities will power and ability to question is what distinguishes us from all other earthly creatures.

Contribution

Courage can only be measured by the outcome of a note worthy and valued purpose. Within each one of us we have the capacity to contribute to society a legacy for good. The freedom we are privileged with as members of humanity is our freedom to apply or neglect our purpose and power for good. We each have a responsibility that when one asks oneself that same question again:

"Staying true to your authentic self and with your specialised skills and knowledge, how can you provide a solution to humanities greatest hopes or fears?"

One has the choice whether to find and practice our spiritual purpose for good and create a greater legacy and vision than what currently exists. From Abraham Lincoln, Robert Owen, and David Livingstone to figures not yet born each must be faced with the choice of what their legacy will be remembered for a force for good or bad. Will your vision be a catalyst for a better society and future for our grand children?

Power

The white ball spirit is an intense source of power due to its resonance with our emotions and passions. For this reason it is closely akin to the female spirit. There is a saying: "Where power is, women are not. Women must be willing to be powerful. Because we bear the scars from the ways men have used their power over us, women often want no part of power." Society needs women and others marginalised and discriminated in society to find the courage to defend their place in society and embrace power. Only once women are prepared to be truly authentic will change come. We must not adopt men's power or become simply stereotype copies of men, but embrace female power and be our true selves. Like the white ball we will then be revealed as a new force in society, culture and economics and an influence to demand equality and balance.

New style of Leadership

"My vision, my hope is simply this: that many business leaders will come to see a primary role of business as incubators of the human spirit, rather than factories for the production of more material goods & services." The essence of the White ball once integrated with the Black Box is to obtain a balance between that which humanity is created from an equal balance of the material and spiritual. An absence or domination of one thinking over the other is a product void of spirituality, humanity and soul or a product of complete chaos, disorder and undirected logic and thinking.

Only once society has learned to respect the source and purpose of both our material and spiritual needs will society find a source of happiness and contentment.

Summary

I. Courage

II. Equality

III. Breaking Rules

IV. Contribution

V. Power

VI. New style of Leadership

Chapter 17

The Time Machine

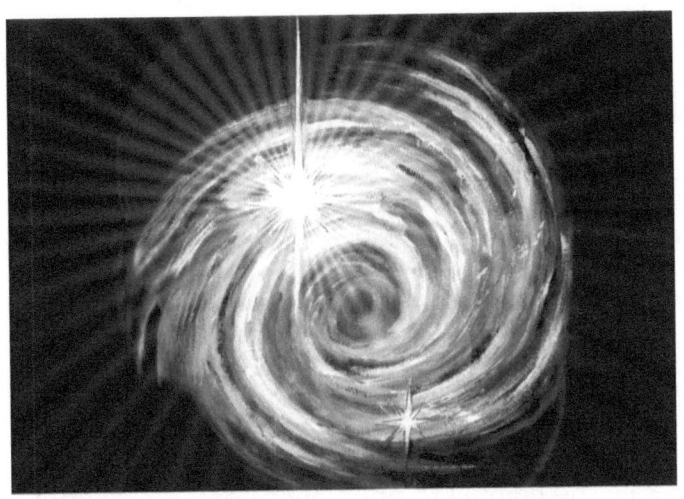

Annie and I entered the last exhibition of the Creativity Centre the 'Time Machine' and made our way to our individual simulator seats in the theatre. Before the 5-D ride began I engaged my seat restraint as my headrest helmet moved into place and the room fell in to darkness.

Immediately the room began simulating conditions from hot to cold generating gentle air currents through our helmets. Gradually small bursts of scents filled the room like the musty smell of an aeroplanes air conditioning system. While the chairs vibrated to the sound of a speeding vehicle as if we were being hurled backwards in time, the TV screens within our helmets began generating 3-D images of a flight in space travelling through a worm hole. The Time machine was stimulating our senses to believe we were being taken to another place and point in time, to analyse what had brought us here. The time machine would take us on a journey of past, present and future in the company of the world's greatest visionaries.

The Time Machine hurled us backwards through time at hyper speed stopping briefly in the in the 1990's with James Dyson saying:"

"….But advertising is the way to a very fast, very small profit, in retailing we saw the coming to prominence of a mentality that wanted to sell boring, low profit items at High Volume………that is the Tunnel vision that sees money as makeable, only by selling cheap things by the truckload…Naturally everyone goes for Advertising instead of (Research & Development), & without encouragement, they will continue to do so for ever & Britain will crumble into dust" "The easy credit offered, & easy money sought, by the Thatcher Revolution encouraged selling not making, If the Banks & the city want instant returns then you go out & sell your old products harder & better than before, & you end up, as we did the most feted advertising Industry in the World, & Bugger all else".

Quickly moving forward in time to 2012 to a quick commentary on the challenge of youth unemployment and the UK's 3-4 million small businesses.

"The solution lies not in the big multinationals but in the UK if every company SME employed just one new member of staff" stated Tim Watts Chairman of Per-temps.

We watched the stream of passionate interviews of significant and courageous individuals. Jamie Oliver challenging our government on the food served in our schools to our children and moving forward in time to see the long term positive impact and influence on our children's health another individual reminiscent of the great Dame Anita Roddick and her impact on eradicating child labour and animal testing.

The Time machine jumped back to the 1930's then moving further backwards in time to the 1860's before propelling us forward through the evolving decades of progress. Each time illuminating the outcome of the past on the present and the possibilities and opportunities for the future for politics, the civil rights movement, apartheid, women's rights, child protection, human rights to world peace depicting the progress of civilisation, innovation, technology and economics on our culture & way of life.

The Time machine hurled us forward in time to the 1930's, 1960's, 1990's to 2013 with flashing black and white photographs, broadcasts, lectures and interviews of Abraham Lincoln, Mahatma Gandhi, Martin Luther King, President John F. Kennedy, Nelson Mandela to the inauguration of the 44th President Barack Obama in 2008. Images of the first television Broadcast of the first moon landing, Live Aid, Steve Jobs launch of apples I-pad, the Olympics London 2012, the Scotsman Andy Murray's triumph winning Wimbledon 2013, the first passenger flight to space. Our minds were bombarded by visual references and depictions of defining moments in time.

Finally the time machine slowed momentum and as we exited the worm whole and emerged into outer space we looked down on planet earth. Our journey had come full circle recapturing the message of the inverted atrium with the Angel Clarence and the glittering array of stars illuminating our planet. As we floated in space simulating the weight free environment of a space craft we listened to the voice of Nelson Mandela:

"Our deepest fear is not that we are inadequate. Our deepest fear is that we are powerful beyond measure. It is our light, not our darkness that most frightens us. We ask ourselves ' Who am I to be brilliant, *gorgeous, talented, and fabulous?'* Actually, who are you not to be? You are a child of God. You're playing small doesn't serve the world. There is nothing enlightened about shrinking so that other people won't feel insecure around you. We are all meant to shine, as children do. We are born to make manifest the glory of God that is within us. It is not in some of us, it is in everyone. And as we make our own light shine, we unconsciously give others permission to do the same. As we are liberated from our fear, our presence automatically liberates others."

Once again, one by one the screen filled with a dazzling array of stars growing brighter and stronger by the minute as the ride gradually came to a halt and the theatre filled with light. Annie & I talked as we slowly made our way out of the Time machine exhibition and towards the atrium.

"Annie, the founders of this park understood our hopes for the future would be determined by our current actions and decisions. They understood that it wasn't going to be some quick fix but a long term commitment to our children and grandchildren. As I have told you before our culture became obsessed with materialism and devoid of the creative spirit. Starting with the small things we began to erode our values with small things like unscrupulous call centres and telemarketing companies harassing people in their homes. Then we had the extremes of the banks gambling away our financial resources, internet companies exploiting personal freedom allowing the proliferation and exploitation of societies most vulnerable, our children and women. 'Black box' thinking took over and consumed everything causing a detachment from the spirit. Unlike the black box the white ball principles stem from our human instincts to nurture, preserve and protect our humanity. The core characteristics of the creative spirit are inspiration, faith, ideas, vision, risk and courage without these and the conviction to protect and question our values, principles and ethics we are no different from all other of earthly creatures. Taking a quote from one man who understood the human spirit Mahatma Gandhi said:

"Whenever you are in doubt, apply the following test; recall the face of the poorest and weakest person you may have seen and ask yourself if the step you contemplate is going to be of any use to them".

This same statement applies to every human life we touch and influence in our day to day lives as a consequence of our decisions and intentions. We must fully understand the results of the ripple effect. One single decision in time can be a negative force of destruction like a Tsunami or a positive call for peace and a revolution for positive change. Single individuals like Nelson Mandela, Ganhdi, Abraham Lincoln, and David Livingstone to Dame Anita Roddick shared visions for positive change.

When you finally decide what path you want to take simply remember Annie,

"What is the business of business? To create wealth? To create jobs? To meet the needs of society? Yes. But there is more. The final goal of any human activity, and any business must show us how to be effective, is to create a world of moral order- a world ethics network."

Our lives are reflections of the past and our present will define our future. The lessons of the past will only serve us if we have the courage and conviction to apply them to the present.

Chapter 18

The Future

Annie and I made our way back to the Atrium and took a seat at one of the observation and group assembly stations. We sat together as I looked across the 'World's Creativity Park' for the last time, enjoying all its grandeur and beauty with its beautiful East Wing gardens before reaching into my bag to reveal an old brown leather book and two small leather pouches.

I turned to Annie and grasping her hand gently, I looked at her straight in the eyes.

"Many years ago on my 17th Birthday my grandmother gave me a very precious gift which she inherited from a sincere and distinguished lady. On my 17th Birthday she simply asked that on my eldest grand daughters 17th Birthday I repeat the same honour and pass this gift onto her."

Pausing briefly, "It seems so long ago but it was such a significant day in my life I can remember that day and moment so vividly it seems like just yesterday. Annie you would have loved my grand mother, she was such an inspiring woman. I have thought about this day for many years from the first moment I held you in my arms and through the years of watching you grow in to a confident young woman. Today I would like to give you this gift and simply ask that on your eldest granddaughters 17th Birthday you repeat the same honour."

"Inside these pouches you will find two paper weights, a white glass ball and a black wooden box." I leant over and opened the small pouch to reveal a white glass ball paper weight and an unusual black box."

Annie looked at her grandmother in amazement, "I always thought that the black box and the white ball was just an old wives tale, an old Scottish myth! ".

I looked at Annie and with a pursed smile slowly shook my head from side to side.

"This book is a book of two valuable teachings, made up of two halves, part one is about *material power* and something known as *black box thinking*, part two is about *creative power* and *white ball thinking*. Its teachings have shaped the lives of those around us. All that I ask is that you embrace the secret of these two principles and allow them to help you in your journey through life as they inspired my Grandmother and me."

"But how did you get the Black Box paper weight?" said Annie curiously.

"Well that's a story for another day……………….." I said smiling mischievously.

Arm in arm Annie & I slowly made our way through the Atrium doors and towards the exit out into a bright sunny afternoon and the invigorating fresh Scottish air.

To be continued………..…..
Part Two: The Black Box
http://www.designovation.co.uk/about

Summary

Part One

"The White Ball Principles"

I The Spirit; Inspiration

I. One must discover and find in life ones single "Creative purpose".

II. Ones ideas must resonate with our values.

III. We must find our place of Natural solitude.

IV. We must find our individual spiritual tools.

V. Detachment tools.

VI. Positive Energy.

VII. Be inspired.

II The Believer; Faith

I. One must be willing to believe anything is possible.

II. Self Belief.

III. Surround yourself with believers.

IV. Test your beliefs.

V. Affirmation & repetition.

III The Inventor; Ideas

I. Believe anything is possible.

II. Focus only on your passion, strength and specialised knowledge.

III. Work & think alone.

IV. Protect 'your' inventor's studio from reality and intruders.

V. Focus on one idea at a time.

VI. Protect you idea from the world until it is complete.

VII. Master Persistence.

VIII. Find new experiences and sources of creative inspiration.

IX. Avoid the company of critics.

X. Acceptance.

WI. Staying true to your authentic self and with your specialised skills and knowledge, how can you provide a solution to humanities greatest hopes or fears?

IV The Designer; Vision

I. The skill to Visualise.

II. Our vision.

III. Dream.

IV. Redesign.

V. The maker.

VI. Strategy.

V The Gambler; Risk

I. Facing fear.

II. Loss of wealth & respect.

III. Calculated Risk.

IV. Certainty.

V. Leaps of faith.

VI The Rebel; Courage

I. Courage.

II. Equality.

III. Breaking Rules.

IV. Contribution.

V. Power.

VI. New style of Leadership.

Notes

Introduction

"The passionate are the only advocates who always persuade. The simplest man with passion will be more persuasive than the most eloquent without." Rene Descartes

Chapter 10

"the greatest sickness in our society is loneliness & if anyone of us has a product or a store that counteracts loneliness we will have a business that will last forever" Dame Anita Roddick

"The wish their heart made". Jiminy Cricket. Disney.

Chapter 12

"The reason why so many people assume that they are incapable of creating images is that, instead of understanding that the brain always succeeds through continued experimentation, they mistake initial failure for fundamental incapacity and as its true measure of their talent. They therefore leave to wither and die a mental skill which could have flourished naturally."

Tony Buzan. "The Mind map Book", BBC. P73.

"We make use of a massive range of cortical skills (brain functions); colour, form, line, dimension, texture, visual rhythm and especially imagination 'To picture mentally'. Images are therefore often more evocative than word, more precise and potent in triggering a wide range of associations, thereby enhancing creative thinking and memory".

Tony Buzan. "The Mind map Book", BBC. P74.

Chapter 14

What do you think it takes to come up with a good invention?

You've got to have a pretty darn good idea in your head of an end goal. You can't just sit down and start using some tools you were taught and see where it takes you. You need one goal, and your goal has to coincide with something that somebody else wants to buy or something that will save them money.

Kenneth A. Brown. "Inventors at work", Steve Wozniak P228

One inventor I talked to said he never tells anyone what he's working on because people can be so negative. Have you ever felt that way?

Exactly, exactly! Right and left! Right and left! Right and left! And I put up with it. I'm really patient and nice to people. But it's hard when you have an idea and you want to implement it the way you see it and everyone else tells you why it won't work.

Kenneth A. Brown. "Inventors at work", Steve Wozniak P229

Do you usually work alone?

Anything that I've ever been proud of or was acknowledged for later was always done on my own. For example , I wrote one set of code release for a custom microprocessor two summers ago when my wife was in Europe with the kids…..As it turned out during those three weeks with just enough time alone and away from the family, I got a ton of work done. I could go for a year trying to get done what I accomplished in those three weeks.

Kenneth A. Brown. "Inventors at work", Steve Wozniak .P230

"I knew I was going to be an engineer from day one….There's a certain window in your life when you're very young and you get a few things in your hands. And then, for the rest of your life, they're familiar and they're friends and that's your thing. If you got a car that you started working on in seventh grade, you'd probably be working on cars for the rest of your life."

Kenneth A. Brown. "Inventors at work", Steve Wozniak .P220

"The first requisite for success is to apply your physical and mental energies to one problem incessantly without growing weary " Brian Tracy. "Eat that Frog". John Haggi. Thomas Edison *P71*.

"Concentrate all your thoughts on the task at hand. The suns rays do not burn until brought to a focus "
Brian Tracy. "Eat that Frog". John Haggi. *Alexander Graham Bell. P61.*

"Imagination is everything. It is the preview of Life's coming attractions". Albert Einstein

Chapter 11

"God is in the detail" Great architect Mies van der Rohe.

Chapter 16

"I dream, I test my dreams against my beliefs, I dare to take risks, and I execute my vision to make those dreams come true. Dream, Believe, Dare, Do." Bill Capodagli & Lynn Jackson. "The Disney Way" P125, Walt Disney.

"The leader who dares to take risks is often an outsider who doesn't feel constricted by the establishments rules….. the French impressionist Claude Monet….was ridiculed by the art establishment. Walt Disney…as the producer of cartoons, he was looked upon as small time." Bill Capodagli & Lynn Jackson. "The Disney Way" P125, Walt Disney.

Chapter 17

"Real creativity, the kind that is responsible for breakthrough changes in our society, always violates the rules". Dame Anita Roddick. "Business as Usual", P218 Richard Farson.

"There is a saying: Where power is, women are not. Women must be willing to be powerful. Because we bear the scars from the ways men have used their power over us, women often want no part of power." Dame Anita Roddick. "Business as Usual", P136 Petra Kelly.

"My vision, my hope is simply this: that many business leaders will come to see a primary role of business as incubators of the human spirit, rather than factories for the production of more material goods and services." Dame Anita Roddick. "Business as Usual".P25

Chapter 18

"….But advertising is the way to a very fast, very small profit, in retailing we saw the coming to prominence of a mentality that wanted to sell boring, low profit items at High Volume……….that is the Tunnel vision that sees money as makeable, only by selling cheap things by the truckload…Naturally everyone goes for Advertising instead of (Research & Development), & without encouragement, they will continue to do so for ever & Britain will crumble into dust"

James Dyson. Against all Odds.1997.

"The easy credit offered, & easy money sought, by the Thatcher Revolution encouraged selling not making, If the Banks & the city want instant returns then you go out & sell your old products harder & better than before, & you end up, as we did the most feted advertising Industry in the World, & Bugger all else".

"The solution lies not in the big multinationals but in the UK if every company SME employed just one new member of staff" .BBC interview with *Tim Watts Chairman of Per temps* "Show me the money

"Our deepest fear is not that we are inadequate. Our deepest fear is that we are powerful beyond measure. It is our light, not our darkness that most frightens us. We ask ourselves ' Who am I to be brilliant, gorgeous, talented, fabulous?' Actually, who are you not to be? You are a child of God. You're playing small doesn't serve the world. There is nothing enlightened about shrinking so that other people won't feel insecure around you. We are all meant to shine, as children do. We are born to make manifest the glory of God that is within us. It is not in some of us, it is in everyone. And as we make our own light shine, we unconsciously give others permission to do the same. As we are liberated from our fear, our presence automatically liberates others." Nelson Mandela (Marianne Williamson)

"Whenever you are in doubt, apply the following test; recall the face of the poorest and weakest person you may have seen and ask yourself if the step you contemplate is going to be of any use to them". Dame Anita Roddick. "Business as Usual", P207 Mahatma Gandhi.

"What is the business of business? To create wealth? To create jobs? To meet the needs of society? Yes. But there is more. The final goal of any human activity, and any business must show us how to be effective, is to create a world of moral order- a world ethics network."

Dame Anita Roddick. "Business as Usual", P15 Peter Koestenbaum.

Bibliography

Napoleon Hill. "Your Magic Power to be Rich" The Master Key, P325. Penguin.

Robert Kiosaki. "Rich Dad Poor Dad".

Dame Anita Roddick. "Business as Usual".

Kenneth A. Brown. "Inventors at work", Steve Wozniak Interview.

Bill Capodagli & Lynn Jackson. "The Disney Way" P125, Walt Disney.

BBC interview with Tim Watts Chairman of Per-temps "Show me the money".

Brian Tracy. "Eat that Frog". John Haggi.

Tony Buzan. "The Mind map Book", BBC.

(Influences)

Neal Gabler. "Walt Disney", Vintage.

Norman Vincent Peale. "The Power of Positive Thinking". Cedar

Napoleon Hill. "Think & Grow Rich".Tarcher. Penguin.

Napoleon Hill. Annotated Sharon Lechter. "Outwitting the Devil".Sterling.

Michael.E.Gerber. "The E-Myth revisited". Harper Collins.

James Dyson. Against the Odds. 1997

James Redfield. The Celestine Prophecy. Bantam Books.

Peter Krass. "Carnegie". Wiley.

Sam Walton with John Huey. "Made in America", Bantam Books.

Esther & Jerry Hicks. "Money & The Law of Attraction", Hay House.

"The Richest man in Babylon"

About the Author

D.F. McKeever is a Scottish Author & Illustrator. She lives in Scotland with her husband and three children. Her passion and interest in personal development & studying successful individuals began in her early teens, while pursuing a career and degree in Design. In addition to working in the family business (manufacturing & engineering company) from her early teens she built her own retail & design business, which she operated for 18 years servicing the public & private sector in Scotland.

The inspiration for "Black Box & White Ball Thinking" came from her experiences in attempting to help her husband get an invention to market the "Shoogle". Her dealings with various Enterprise institutions raised fundamental questions to the lack of understanding of what motivates & makes an Entrepreneur. And what is being taught about the operating models we need for enterprise to succeed in the 21st Century and how creativity & innovation are central to its success.

Are you an aspiring Entrepreneur?

Sign-up and receive your FREE Business Start-up Handbook

NOW!

Just visit us at: *http://www.designovation.co.uk*

https://youtu.be/uwp7A3U_5hs

https://twitter.com/dfmckeever